I NEVER SAW IT COMING!

Forty-six Years working in law enforcement

By

Donald R. Smith

I NEVER SAW IT COMING!

Forty-six years working in law enforcement.

By

Donald R. Smith

Senior Special Agent (Retired)

Immigration and Customs Enforcement

U.S. Department of Homeland Security

FIRST PRINTING

Book Writing Consultant has allowed this work to remain exactly as the author intended, verbatim, without editorial input.

FOREWORD

As the cover says, "I Never Saw It Coming." I am talking about retirement, so let's go back to the beginning so I can explain. I have worked numerous jobs throughout my life, and even when I started with the U.S. Border Patrol in 1988, I never dreamed that I would one day have to consider retirement. The way I saw it, I would be dead before I could enjoy anything like retirement.

Honestly, I never thought about retirement, and when people discussed it, I ignored them because I knew I wouldn't make it to retirement age anyway. Understand that most people in my family have died while in their fifties or sixties. My dad passed away at fifty-seven, and my mom at forty-one, and many of my relatives have passed away at an early age on both sides of my family.

So, when it came to work, I always had life insurance through my employment to cover Linda's expenses, but I never planned on having a retirement check for Linda.

However, it occurred to me about ten months before I decided to consider retirement, and at that time, I realized I would retire. I asked myself what I was doing now, whether I was ready, and whether I had done anything that had prepared me for it. I questioned whether I had retirement savings, where they were, and how I would get them.

My problem was that I was caught off guard by the emotion that goes with it, suddenly realizing I would not be making money. I figured I had sufficient retirement capital but wasn't accustomed to spending my money instead of making it. It was scary to shift from earning a regular paycheck to living off your hard-earned savings month after month.

Some of these emotions stemmed from my work ethic, which drove me to be a provider rather than a spender. I am experiencing stress due to the need to replace a paycheck with a retirement check. Well, as it turned out, I was good to go! Luckily, I had set everything up initially, which prepared me well for retirement. I had inadvertently prepared everything without knowing I was doing it or doing it right.

For me, the thought of retirement was challenging enough without the added fear and stress of not knowing what would happen when I retired.

As it turned out, I was prepared and ready for retirement, but it's funny that after all those years of me thinking and believing.

I wouldn't ever retire, here I am. I never took the time to prepare myself for retirement properly, but here I am at the ten-month mark before retirement. It finally hit me: retirement was here. I will officially retire from the government and not work and then see if my checks come in as planned. I didn't die, so now I am facing retirement. "I never saw it coming!"

Dedication

"I Never Saw It Coming" is written about my lifetime career in law enforcement, drawn from a collection of family memories, pictures, well-kept records, and years of journaling, culminating in my retirement on December 31, 2022.

This takes you through all the years of love and laughter with my wife, Linda, of fifty years, and my son, Jacob, who is about to turn forty-seven. It also includes the struggles of moving from place to place and the occasional job-related stresses.

It's a journey filled with hard work and sacrifices that I am proud and blessed to have accomplished, but not without the unending support of my family, who were always willing to take the next step with me wherever I took them.

With that being said, it's with much love for their support and our years of memories that I dedicate this book with love to:

Linda and Jacob Smith

Table of Contents

Introduction

This is about me, Donald R. Smith, "Donnie," and my family following a forty-six (46) year law enforcement career. I will discuss the "trials and tribulations," referring to the challenges we, as a family, endure that test our faith, love, hope, and more. I will cover the period from the moment we start this venture until we reach the finish line, marking retirement. The Bible says in James 1:2-3 to consider it joy when encountering various trials, "knowing that the testing of your faith produces endurance."

On December 31, 2022, I retired after a forty-six-year career in law enforcement. Throughout my career, I have held positions within local police departments and collaborated with federal law enforcement agencies across the United States. In every position I have held, I have made a concerted effort to learn every aspect of that role to enhance my career and better provide for my family.

My career began as a police officer for the Amite City Police Department in Amite, Louisiana. It progressed to the Baton Rouge City Police Department (BRPD), where I held various positions, including Police Officer, Detective, Homicide, Narcotics Agent, and Motorcycle Officer. From the BRPD, I entered federal law enforcement service. I held positions as a U.S. Border Patrol Agent, Immigration Inspector, Senior Immigration Inspector, Special Operations Officer, Supervisory Immigration Inspector, Area Port Director, Officer in Charge, and Supervisory Special Agent. I retired as a Senior Special Agent.

One of the most complex decisions I have ever made was to retire in December 2022. I did not have to retire, but I always said I would know when the time was right. Around June 2022, I realized it was approaching that time. I had to first convince myself of it, and once I did, turning in my retirement papers was the next hurdle to overcome.

Now, I will admit that after submitting my retirement package for processing, everything seemed to become easier for me regarding acceptance.

I have decided to document these positions and locations on

paper. I encountered many engaging experiences and wanted to share them with my wife, Linda, and son, Jacob. I want to believe that I am writing this for my family, but I am also writing this for myself because, after working for forty-six years, I now want to put everything into perspective. I kept daily ledgers throughout my career, attempting to document my involvement and everything else. The more I reviewed my journals, the more I realized how lucky. I was to have experienced so many things, good and bad.

During my career, Linda, Jacob, and I have lived in cities around the United States while working in various law enforcement fields. Now, I want to slow down and absorb everything I experience, trying to put it on paper for my family to read.

Being able to write this gives me an outlet and something to occupy my time. Over the years, I have found that writing about my experiences is quite therapeutic. Reviewing my notes, journals, and photo albums evokes a multitude of fond memories.

My writing is about overcoming adversity, and on many occasions, I could have easily chosen the wrong path and ended up in a career other than law enforcement.

My forty-six-year career has passed quickly, and the memories have already begun to fade away. Luckily, I have my handwritten daily journals, which I kept for most of my adult life. I often refer to them to recollect my past at any given time. Retiring was a difficult decision. Regardless of why I decided to retire, I will always miss the camaraderie among my fellow agents the most. I always knew that at some point, I had to prepare myself to become a regular citizen. That loss of power and no longer being a part of the "family" will require significant adjustments for me, and leaving this sort of protection was not easy for me to do.

I must confess that I could not have had my lengthy career without Linda's love and support. She never complained and always went with the flow.

Moving around the country and working in new positions to learn was challenging, but it was only possible because I had a loving wife who supported me and my career.

She was willing to step aside and let me pass, creating a pathway for our future.

When we arrived at our new duty locations, I would learn about the details of my new office while Linda learned about the city streets and where everything was located. The most important things for her were finding grocery stores, a doctor's office, and schools for Jacob. At the time, she used only a city map because, back then, there was no Waze or Google Maps to help her.

Linda was a great mom. She took excellent care of Jacob while adjusting to an unfamiliar environment and managing our household and financial situation. I may have earned the paycheck, but Linda managed our bills by moving money around and sometimes doing a little magic to make ends meet. I don't know what I would have done without her and her financial abilities. I told many people I could bring a nickel home today, and Linda would turn it into a dime by tomorrow. Linda is the smartest person I know, and I trust her with everything.

Poor Jacob had to move from city to city and change schools until graduating high school. But he always managed to adjust and made the best of every situation. He made friends wherever he went, played on baseball teams, and even got a job working while attending school. I hope moving around so much has helped him cope with the demanding situations and adjust to unfamiliar environments. Hopefully, his experiences have helped him become the man he is today. Linda and I are extremely proud of him and the man he has become.

Linda and Jacob, I apologize for all the inconvenience I have caused you. Every decision I made was made with the betterment of all three of us in mind. I always worked so hard to give you everything you needed. But you must admit, as it turned out, "we" didn't do too badly in life, and I could never express my gratitude to you both for the sacrifices you made for me.

I hope all who read this will understand the sacrifices, commitments, and heartaches we went through to cross that finish line as a happy family and know that our accomplishments were well-deserved and earned!

Chapter 1
Donald Ray Smith

I was born in October 1956 in New Orleans, Louisiana. My parents were Norman Smith and Eva Wiley Smith. They had four children, with me being the "firstborn," as my dad always called me.

We lived in New Orleans until around the summer of 1968. Before that summer, my dad had a severe heart attack, forcing him to retire early.

Dad was a machinist working at Dibert Bancroft and Ross. We eventually left New Orleans and moved to Kentwood, LA, near Dad's family, where he was born and raised. Dad needed to get out of the city and into a calmer atmosphere with less stress.

We rented a small house on Highway 38 until Mom and Dad

eventually built a new house on Highway 38 West, near the New Zion Church and elementary school.

I attended New Zion Elementary before Greensburg High School in Greensburg, Louisiana, and we also participated in activities at New Zion Baptist Church.

I graduated from Greensburg High School in 1975, and I would love to say that I graduated with high honors and was at the top of my class, but that would be a lie. I was one of those who barely got by and prayed a lot when exams came around. While attending high school, I lettered in football and joined the Future Farmers of America (FFA). I still have my football and FFA jackets.

In October 1974, several of us from the school traveled to Amite to obtain supplies for repairing the glass windows in the agriculture building. When the windows got broken or minor repairs were needed around the school, we seniors did what we could to repair or replace items as needed and save the school money.

While in Amite, we stopped at the TG&Y (Toys, Games, and Yoyos) store on Hwy 16, west of town. Although the store no longer exists, it was the go-to destination for everything at the time.

In TG&Y, I was walking around the store when I saw this

pretty girl with long, dark hair walking toward me. I remember thinking how pretty she was and how I could talk to her. Before I realized it, she walked up to me and asked if I was Donnie, and then she introduced herself as Linda. To my surprise, she was a friend of my brother's girlfriend.

My brother's girlfriend and Linda attended Valley Forge Academy, a private school outside Amite. After talking for a while and using my charm, I asked her for a date, and she agreed. Linda gave me her home phone number, and I was so excited because she was gorgeous and I knew I wanted to be with her.It took me several weeks to finally talk with her and discuss our date. I later learned from her mom that she was hiding from me and did not want to take my phone calls. Luckily, she gave in to my harassment and stalking and went on that date with me. See, it goes to show that being persistent can pay off. It did for me! Thank you, God!

Linda and I dated for approximately 10 months before she said yes and married me on September 12, 1975. Our wedding was held at the Beulah Baptist Missionary Church in Bolivar, LA. I remember talking with my dad one night and telling him I wanted to ask Linda to marry me. He said, "Son, she's a keeper." That was good enough for me, and I went for it.

Pastor Mason Miley from Beulah Church presided, and he later became a good friend throughout the years. Bro. Miley helped us move from the house we rented on Highway 16 in Amite to our first house, which we purchased on Ellis Road in Amite. That man never hesitated to lend a hand when needed. He and I went on several fishing trips and had nice talks.

Linda and I have one son, Jacob Norman Smith, named after my dad, Norman. Most of Jacob's friends call him Jake. Jacob attended numerous elementary schools, high schools, and colleges. Jacob became the son any man could ever wish for. Today, I am enormously proud of him and all his accomplishments.

Most importantly, he is his own man and makes his own decisions dealing with life, but his mom and I were always there for him. Although he made his own decisions, I always stood right behind him, watching his every step. I wasn't going to let him fall.

Below is Linda and me from our wedding.

On the right is our first house, which we purchased in Amite for $37,500. While waiting for a closing date, I worked for the Amite Police Department. Working the night shift, I would ride by the house at around 3:00 a.m., staring at it, wondering how we would pay the mortgage. But I was also proud of us for purchasing the house because we were starting a family, and this would be our new home.

Since September 12, 1975, Linda and I have been together through good and challenging times, but we have always found a way to work things out and make sense of them. That takes commitment, and we both gave as much of that as we could.

With all the work transfers and moving around the country, Linda never once complained. She was always supportive and encouraged me in every move I made.

From the beginning, Linda supported me with the Amite Police, the Baton Rouge City Police, and federal law enforcement. How do you express gratitude for that? I can't thank her enough for all her support, encouragement, and sacrifices. I don't know where we would have ended up if it were not for her.

Linda was more than a wife and mother; she managed our family finances and, basically, our lives. I could tell stories about what Linda went through financially to keep our heads above water. I have to hand it to her—she did it!

She hung in there with me and never once tried to discourage me. When I would come home and tell her that we were moving to another city, she was always supportive and never discouraged me.

I questioned many of my decisions, but always relied on my gut feeling. I weighed my options and prayed that I would make the right decision. The Lord was good to us by leading us in the right direction.

Reflecting on the most pivotal moments in my career makes me realize how incredibly different the outcomes could have been if I hadn't taken the time to consider my decisions. Wisdom has reinforced that a gut instinct should be factored into any decision-making process.

We often go through life unaware of the feelings, thoughts, emotions, and sensations that drive our actions. During the day, we make numerous decisions, such as when to get out of bed, what to eat, how to organize our time, how to engage with others, and what behavior is right or wrong.

I believe that all of these decisions shape our reality, identity, and life story. What if I had not taken that position in Atlanta and decided to stay in Miami? What if I had never gone to Miami and stayed in Houston?

Linda and I's decisions throughout our careers formed and molded our lives, bringing us to where we are today. But still, even today, I often wonder, what if... Pictured are Jacob, Me, and Linda.

CHAPTER 2

Amite City Police Department

After graduating from Greensburg High School, I began working in August 1975 as a tack welder at Avondale Shipyard, located in New Orleans on the Mississippi River. I recall being offered a job with a salary of $3.50 per hour as a tack welder. That was a relatively decent amount of money to earn graduating from high school at the time. Besides, I needed the job because Linda and I were getting married in September, and I knew we couldn't get married without my having a steady income. The day I was hired at Avondale was exciting, and I couldn't wait to get home and tell Linda all about it. We didn't have cell phones back then, so I had to wait until I got home.

We worked outside most of the time, and if it rained heavily, we couldn't work.

On a rainy day, sometime in May 1976, I was off work because we could not weld in the rain. I was sitting around our apartment at 100 W. Pine Street in Amite, and while sitting there, I decided to do something I had been thinking about for some time. I had always wondered what it would be like to be a police officer for the Amite City Police Department (APD). I recall watching police vehicles drive around town and wondering what it would be like to work in that profession.

Although I had given considerable thought to being a police officer, I never mentioned my desire to anyone and didn't even discuss it with Linda.

I had never met or known any of the officers, so I had no one to discuss the position with.

On that rainy day, I decided to drive to Amite City Town Hall and apply. At that time, the APD's primary office was behind the City Hall building, so I parked and went inside. The office was an exceedingly small room with only a counter and one desk.

Upon entering the office, I met a lady who identified herself as

Ms. Norris Ellzey, stating that she was the APD police clerk and dispatcher. I told Ms. Ellzey of my intentions, so she provided me with an employment application. She told me that if I wanted, I could complete the application there and leave it with her or take it home. I decided to complete the application there, and I left it with her. She briefly looked it over and told me someone may contact me later.

While preparing my application at the counter, I noticed a white male police officer sitting in a chair, reading a newspaper by the desk, and occasionally watching me. He never said anything to me, but watched me as I filled out the application. When I left the building, he was still sitting in the chair, reading the newspaper.

As I left the office and drove home, I remembered thinking this was all a waste of time because no one would contact me.

I genuinely wanted to be a police officer, work in my hometown, and join the community.

One aspect I considered was the salary of a police officer in Amite. I knew it would not be good, but I would give it a chance anyway because I was truly committed. I knew or had already decided I would not hesitate to accept the position if given the opportunity.

I drove back to our apartment and pulled into the driveway. I walked into the apartment and told Linda I had applied with the APD. Surprisingly, she was supportive, although she knew the salary would not be as good as I was earning at Avondale. That was the first time Linda supported me in my venture into law enforcement. She never discouraged me in any way.

Not long after I got home, there was a knock on the front door. When I went to the door, the same police officer who was at City Hall watching me fill out my application was now standing in my doorway. He immediately identified himself as Chief J.C. Ricks and stated that he had reviewed my application, inquiring whether I was interested in becoming a member of the APD. I told him I was, and we sat on the front porch talking about police work.

After speaking with him for a while, he suggested I ride along as a reserve officer to see if I would like performing this job before making my final decision. Also, riding as a reserve would allow me to experience what it's like to be a police officer and determine if it's something I want to pursue as a career. The Chief said we could talk about a full-time position after I work some time as a reserve.

When the Chief suggested that I

become an auxiliary police officer, I hoped it was my chance to secure a full-time position. So, I immediately began riding with the other officers, learning as much as possible about everything.

I devoted myself to the auxiliary program and worked for approximately five months before being hired as a full-time police officer.

Although we all worked hard, we found time to unwind and have fun on numerous occasions, as that was when camaraderie existed in my career. We all knew one another and considered each other family. In today's law enforcement, camaraderie means nothing and does not exist in many places.

Chief Ricks provided me with the necessary tools for the job, including a badge, credentials, uniform, gun belt, and accessories. The APD did not supply a service weapon, so I had to provide my own. It was an S&W Model 19, .357 caliber, a six-shot revolver, and an outstanding weapon for law enforcement. I bought the weapon from Thompson's Sporting Goods in Amite on Main Street.

Linda provided me with a small wooden chair beside the bed in our bedroom. While not working, I hung my gun belt and uniform on the chair. I also kept all the police-related items on that chair, such as assorted paperwork, traffic violation codes, criminal codes I was trying to learn, and numerous other minor items.

In the mornings, on my way out the door to Avondale, I looked at that chair, and I knew I had an opportunity; all I needed was time. That chair and its belongings represented a future for me, and I became proud of that chair and all the items hanging on it.

In December 1976, I remember that night at the city council meeting when Chief Ricks recommended that I be hired full-time as a police officer. All the city council members agreed to hire me, which made me proud because I did not know any of them personally.

It was not until after I was hired that I learned Linda's uncle, Tilman T. Alford, had been a police officer for the APD in the 1960s. Everyone called him Tebo for short. While on duty, he carried an S&W .38 Special, six-shot weapon, and I still have that weapon today. Linda's mom had the weapon, and she gave it to me to keep.

Amite Police Station

When I started, our police station was a small, cinderblock building with no jail cells. It was located on the southeast corner of Hwy 51 and Hwy 16 downtown, next to the railroad tracks. The main police office was still behind the City Hall building.

The APD operated out of this small building for approximately 18 years before relocating to the new police station, inside the renovated train depot across the street.

I had read that Amite City received a federal grant that allowed the renovation of the old depot to become a new police station. This new station features jail cells, a kitchen, a radio room, a Chief's Office, and numerous other offices for staff to work out of.

Amite City purchased the depot for $30,000 in 1975 and spent $22,000 renovating it for the APD's use. In January 1979, the depot was completed, and the APD moved from across the street into the new police station. Not long after we moved into the building, a photograph was taken of officers standing before our new police station.

The new station provided us with the space to perform our duties properly and to place someone in a city jail cell without needing to go to the Tangipahoa Parish Sheriff's Office jail for booking procedures.

The new station had several rooms for processing suspects and conducting interviews and interrogations as needed. When it came to preparing traffic accident reports, we had a place to go and properly prepare and draft them. Our dispatcher was now in the same building with us, allowing us to obtain information more quickly and receive better assistance.

Officer Jeff Austin was a huge inspiration in my law enforcement career. Jeff was an older gentleman who had retired from the Baton Rouge Police Department (BRPD) before coming to work in Amite.

Jeff was the type of guy who kept to himself and never got involved in anyone's business. He always worked the late shift at night, getting off duty at 6:00 a.m. each morning.

While working night shifts, Jeff and I would ride around town together, and he would tell me stories from when he worked for the BRPD. Some of the stories he told intrigued me, making me consider the possibility of working for the BRPD myself. When I asked him a question about police work, he would provide incredibly detailed explanations and was very descriptive in his attempts to help me understand. I still don't understand why he was never used more in training other officers.

Jeff's stories intrigued me enough to consider possibly working for the BRPD. Jeff spoke to me about the training he received and the type of work he performed while with the BRPD, explaining how the work shifts operated. He often discussed the BRPD with me, and I eventually expressed interest in working there. Jeff always listened to me, but he never encouraged me or discouraged me in any way. He said that decisions like going to work for BRPD were my decisions and that I should not let anyone influence me.

Eventually, I talked with Chief Ricks, telling him I wanted to explore the possibility of working for the BRPD. Although I was waiting for the laughter to start, the Chief said I should pursue it if that were what I wanted. The Chief said he would not try to hold me back but encouraged me to pursue my ambitions. I remember him telling me that I probably would not stay long and that I would want to pursue other avenues.

I remember telling everyone else in the department about my ambitions, and to my surprise, everyone was encouraging, but they also expressed their sadness that I would be leaving. Honestly, at one point, I almost changed my mind and stayed with APD, thinking I had a decent job and was right at home. Chief Ricks gave me my start in law enforcement, and who knows what I might be doing now if he hadn't believed in me?

Jeff instilled in me the desire to explore a law enforcement career with the BRPD and initially convinced me to pursue it. I will be forever grateful to him.

Old Amite Police Station

My Uniform Patch

That little building had enough working space for two people, although three officers could sit and talk. A small restroom at the rear had a toilet and a sink. That was it! When shift change came around, we all stood outside by the cars and discussed anything important the next shift might need to know. There was no jail cell, so when someone was arrested, they were transported to the Tangipahoa Parish jail, which was then located at the old courthouse.

Below is the new police station, located in the former Amite depot. We moved into it in January 1979. This new station gave us the room to perform our duties properly and put someone in a city jail without going to the Tangipahoa Parish Sheriff's Office jail.

As I previously stated, Chief JC Ricks gave me my start in law enforcement, and I am incredibly appreciative because if not for him, I would not have had a long forty-six-year career.

I still remember that rainy day when I filled out the application in the office, standing at the counter. I remember being a little nervous and anxious, trying to figure out who the officer was and not saying a word. I remember going home and thinking it was all a waste of time and effort because the APD would not hire me. I also wondered how I would tell Linda that I submitted my application.

I was told and learned that the job is what you make it. I didn't let other people's attitudes or opinions influence me, and I admit that there were officers and policies that I didn't like or agree with in Amite. But with the Lord's blessings, it all came together, and I knew I was on my way to a great law enforcement career.

I left the APD in June 1979 after two and a half years to further my career in the academy with the Baton Rouge Police Department.

CHAPTER 3

Baton Rouge City Police (BRPD)

Well, I did it. I said my goodbyes to everyone at APD and received well-wishes, good luck, and pats on my back. On my last day as an APD officer, I gathered my belongings and looked around the station. I remember thinking I didn't want to burn any bridges because I might have to come back. So, I ensured I was on solid ground with everyone, including Chief Ricks, in case I had to come crawling back.

Leaving the APD was not easy. It was hard for me because I had made so many friends and was starting to feel like I was positively impacting my community. Moving from the APD to the BRPD was a step up for me, but I had to ensure my decision was made with sound reasoning and careful consideration.

I remember saying goodbye to everyone and feeling a profound sense of emptiness. I had many good memories there and knew I would never lose them. The good memories will live with me and hopefully help shape my future. I recall using those memories as a source of comfort and strength when I began the academy. Each person I said goodbye to became a personal story, reminding me of my connections with them. Every person I worked with created memories that reminded me of how changes can lead to new beginnings. What would I have done if I had never met Jeff Alston and talked about the BRPD?

When we think about saying goodbye, it's essential to remember the beautiful moments that come with it. They enrich our lives and give us the courage to take the next step, knowing we carry fragments of those experiences wherever we go.

I just hoped the BRPD was a place where I could continue that search for knowledge to build on and find more.

I genuinely wanted to do more, and I knew that working with the BRPD would increase my responsibility for maintaining public safety, enforcing laws, and protecting a larger community. I understand that the officers at BRPD also played a crucial role in preventing and responding to all sorts of criminal activities, ensuring the well-being of individuals and their property.

My choice to work for BRPD hinged on my potential for longevity. I saw room for growth, advancement, and/or promotion. I saw an opportunity for special assignments within the department, and I wanted an environment that utilized my skills and abilities. I wanted to feel wanted and to have a place to call home.

I hoped the BRPD would offer me various duties, including patrolling assigned areas, responding to emergency calls, conducting investigations, making arrests, and issuing citations or warnings for law violations.

After speaking with numerous individuals and conducting research, I applied for the BRPD. After applying on April 16, 1979, I took the Baton Rouge Police Civil Service Test and passed. To make a long story short, in June 1979, I attended the twelve-week BRPD

academy in Baton Rouge. The academy was extensive, consisting of basic law enforcement training in criminal and civil law for city and state personnel, as well as comprehensive firearms training, physical fitness training, and self-defense training.

On August 29, 1979, at 2:00 p.m., I graduated from the 40th Session of the BRPD academy. We were fortunate that all the Baton Rouge City Council members, Mayor W.W. Dumas, and the BRPD Chief George Johnston attended our graduation.

My First Assignment

On August 22, 1979, I received my first official orders with the BRPD, which instructed me to report to the Uniform Patrol Division at Winbourne Station, located on Winbourne Avenue, on September 4, 1979, at 9:45 p.m. I was so excited and empowered, like a bona fide police officer ready to conquer the city of Baton Rouge. Working in uniform patrol was an excellent start, and I learned greatly from the officers assigned there.

While working in uniform patrol, I attempted to learn everything I could about every aspect of police work. I rode with several training partners and watched, listened, and learned much from them. It was extremely exciting because even though I was once an APD officer, it didn't compare to what I was experiencing with the BRPD.

Working in uniform patrol was an enjoyable experience

because we responded to a wide range of police calls, including home burglaries, car thefts, disturbance calls, and even bar fights, to name a few.

During the police academy, I became friends with one of the instructors, Sgt. Bruce Waymire, and I would discuss everything from working hard to building a good reputation and advancing in the ranks. He told me that, given my previous experience, I should learn things more quickly and advance up the ranks easily. I once expressed my desire to become a detective and conduct criminal investigations, and he laughed, telling me to be patient and that it could happen in time. Sgt. Waymire told me he liked me because I was a young man from a small police department trying to better myself in life and in every way. I trusted him greatly and often called and spoke with him whenever I had questions about the department.

Special Police Operations Team (SPOT)

I learned that the BRPD had a specialized SPOT that focused solely on investigating burglaries and thefts. The detectives assigned to that unit were trained in investigating home and vehicle burglaries. After inquiring about that unit, many officers told me that you would typically need around five years of police experience before you would be given any thought of being assigned to that unit.

It was sometime in October 1979 when I received a phone call from Sgt. Waymire telling me to write a letter to Sgt. Burns, who supervised SPOT, to request an official transfer to that unit. He explained that there was an opening and thought it would be a suitable place for me to enter as a detective and gain more experience. So, I wrote the transfer request letter and submitted it to Sgt. Burns for his consideration, and within a few days, he called me on the phone to schedule an interview at the SPOT office.

On the day of my interview, I met Sgt. Burns, who turned out to be an extremely nice guy, and we talked for a long time. He asked me many questions about my experience working for the APD and what I wanted to do in the future. I answered his questions and felt I had explained everything clearly. After leaving the interview, I felt good about it, but I also knew the other two candidates had more experience.

Unexpectedly, Sgt. Burns called me about a week later to welcome me to the unit and said I should receive a transfer letter from the chief shortly.

On November 1, 1979, I reported for my first day of duty at SPOT. I was assigned to investigate residential and vehicle burglaries.

Special Assignment to Narcotics

On February 4, 1980, I received notice of being assigned to the BRPD narcotics unit, where I was tasked with undercover operations. I was to seek out and purchase narcotics from identified targets, and the detail was to last until April 1, 1980.

Stabbed in the Right Knee

Often, detectives from the SPOT and narcotics units would gather together to conduct an operation or sweep the streets. As a group, we would visit city areas and observe people spending time together on street corners. We would stop and approach these individuals for identification purposes to check for outstanding warrants or if they had drugs on their person.

On March 29, 1984, at 8:20 p.m., while performing a group operation, we were working in the 1400 block of Thomas Delpit Street, attempting to make several arrests of individuals for narcotic violations and other charges. I encountered a Black male standing by himself, later identified as Gerald Wayne Adams, and I began talking with

him, attempting to identify him. I told him I was going to conduct a body search, and when I began to search him for weapons and or illegal drugs, he refused to cooperate with me and attempted to leave the area by walking away from me. I grabbed him, placing him under arrest, and he began assaulting me by punching me in the

head, neck, and back area while he was attempting to run away. I grabbed him, and we began fighting. When I grabbed him, turning him upside down,

I was holding his legs in the air with his hands down at my legs. I was preparing to throw him over to the side when I felt a sharp pain in the center of my right knee, and I immediately fell to the ground with him lying on top of me.

It was extremely painful, and I was going in and out of consciousness. At one point, I awoke and discovered other agents staring over me. As I lay there, I heard the siren of an ambulance in the background, and I was taken to the Baton Rouge General Hospital, where I was diagnosed with a deep puncture wound to the right knee. At the time, I felt nothing from my knee to my foot. When I tried to stand up, I had no control over my right leg and couldn't put any pressure on my right foot.

I met with Dr. Steven Wilson, an orthopedic surgeon who

eventually performed surgery on my knee. He discovered that the tendons were cut in half and required complete repair. After the surgery, I stayed in the hospital for a few days before being released to go home. It took months for my knee to heal, and eventually, I returned to work in the narcotics unit.

That night, the officers with me on the scene arrested Adams and charged him appropriately. However, he later pleaded guilty to lesser charges and was released on probation.

Permanent Transferred to Narcotics

On July 23, 1984, I was reassigned permanently to the Narcotics Unit. I was first assigned to continue my previous work as an undercover agent and was instructed to maintain my current approach.

As far as the work was concerned, nothing changed, and I continued the work as I was doing before being permanently assigned to narcotics.

After several years of working in narcotics, I came to realize that I needed a break from the drugs and working the bars and clubs. I decided I wanted to learn other things or do something different that would change my life.

I had worked in several different police positions, but I had never ridden motorcycles for the police department. I have always wanted to ride motorcycles for the BRPD, and I used to watch motorcyclists riding around the city. It looked pretty cool to me, so I decided to try it.

I eventually inquired with several supervisors and spoke with several motorcycle officers to gain their insight into the position. I filled out the necessary papers and officially returned my request to transfer to the Traffic Division, Motorcycle Unit. I thought that doing this would be a big relief for me, as far as stress goes, and would allow me to do something else besides buying drugs.

Motorcycle Division

Not long after considering it, an opening became available in the motorcycle unit. I wrote up my transfer request and turned it over to the Captain of the Traffic Division. I waited a while and never heard anything, so I assumed they had selected someone else to fill the position.

In late July, I was surprised by a request to come to the traffic division for an interview and to take a motorcycle driving test. I attended that interview, completed the motorcycle test and the written examination at the office. A supervisor told me I would be notified if selected.

On August 1, 1985, I received notice that I was chosen to fill the position, and eventually, I transferred to the Motorcycle Division. I later found that riding motors was a blast, and I was proud to have the opportunity to ride for the department. It turned out to be a fabulous change of pace for me, and although I didn't have the stress of doing drug deals, I now have the stress of dealing with traffic around the city.

Return to Uniform Patrol

After working as a burglar detective, undercover narcotics, motorcycles, and general detective work, I wanted to do something else. I thought about returning to uniform patrol, and after thinking about it for a while, I convinced myself to do it.

On January 1, 1986, I left the traffic division, gave up my motorcycle, and transferred to the uniform patrol division on Coursey Blvd, known as the 3rd District. My lieutenant there was Ted Simmons, also from the Amite area. Over time, he and I became good friends and went to dinner with our wives. Remember that I started in uniform patrol at Winborn Station but didn't work there long before being transferred to

SPOT. Therefore, returning to uniform patrol would allow me to gain experience I didn't acquire at Winborn.

In the Uniform Patrol Division, you were responsible for patrolling an area in your assigned district within the city, responding to calls from citizens, conducting preliminary investigations of all types of crimes, and enforcing both criminal and traffic laws.

Over the years I spent with BRPD, I attended numerous training seminars, schools, and classes, including those offered by the Scientific Crime Investigators Institute, Interview and Interrogation Schools, firearms classes, and various law enforcement training programs.

BRPD PAL Boxing

Working for the BRPD allowed me to join the Police Athletic League (PAL) and participate in the boxing program in my spare time.

I started with the PAL boxing team in 1982, and we traveled around, competing in three-round amateur fights at police events and tournaments throughout the state.

I also joined a boxing club in Loranger, LA., called the Skeet Hewitt Boxing Club at the Loranger Coliseum. Joining that club allowed me to fight in matches on Saturday nights. (I'm in a blue shirt.)

I could schedule matches as many times as I wanted each Saturday night. There were nights when I had three fights lined up, but most of the time, it was two. (Right is me and Jacob)

On March 11, 12, and 13, 1983, I boxed in the Louisiana State Golden Glove tournament at the 165 lb. weight class held in Lafayette, LA. I made it to the finals and was scheduled to fight the previous champion from 1982. I won that fight by a technical knockout (TKO) twenty-eight seconds into the first round. I had two good boxing coaches, Buddy and Danny Ridgell, from Tickfaw, LA. I also had Jacob, who collected my trophies after each fight. I don't know how he would have acted if I had lost a fight and not received a trophy. I remember when I had a match, and as soon as it was over, Jacob was in the ring looking for that trophy to collect.

Great River Road Fun Run

At right is a photo of Linda and Jacob running in the Great River Road Run V 1983. It was a one-mile fun run, and Jacob made it the entire mile. I was working the day of the run and drove over to meet them.

While I worked, Linda was great at getting Jacob involved in different events. Not only did Jacob become involved in baseball, but Linda hand-sewed all his Halloween costumes to wear, ensuring Jacob always had a good birthday and Christmas. Jacob is fortunate to have Linda as a mom. I worked a lot and couldn't participate in activities as much as I would have liked. My comfort was Linda because I knew she was always there.

U.S. Border Patrol

After spending over nine years with the BRPD, I began considering a career in federal law enforcement. I applied for the U.S. Marshal Service and the U.S. Border Patrol. At the time, these were the only agencies hiring. When I first applied to these agencies, I didn't receive much support from any of my friends in the police department, except for Captain Don Buller, who was working in the 3rd District. Don and I became good friends while working together, and we often got together with our wives for dinner or parties. Don and his wife supported Linda after I left and started working for the federal government.

I never understood why, but Don was the only real support I received from everyone at BRPD. I knew no one wanted me to leave BRPD because I was secure there, and everyone felt I was giving up my job security for something I knew nothing about. But Don was the one who told me to go for it and not to listen to everyone around the station.

Even after leaving for the Border Patrol Academy, Don and his wife, Leah, checked on Linda and Jacob to ensure everything was all right with them. Don and Leah also visited us when assigned to Houston and Miami. I appreciate Don and Leah's support of Linda, me, and Jacob.

In May 1988, I began training at the U.S. Border Patrol Academy and was subsequently stationed in Marfa, Texas.

CHAPTER 4

Changes in Law Enforcement

I discovered that law enforcement, in every aspect, is constantly evolving, and so are the people occupying those positions. Working years in law enforcement can make you bitter, skeptical, and even distrustful of people. But what makes you this way? The public thinks that the police have a solution for every problem. Law enforcement officers are not immune to societal changes, and I was exposed to the misery and conflict that people face in their lives, which gave me a more nuanced view of the people.

People in law enforcement know that you cannot deny reality because it could get you severely injured or even killed. After a while, I could no longer look at things the way I used to because now, when I go somewhere, I constantly scan my surroundings, look for exits, and remain continuously alert. I chose a seat with my back to the wall and a view of the entire place. I even feel uncomfortable without my weapon and badge, as everything seems suspicious, no matter where I go, until I can prove otherwise.

Over time, the job has influenced sites, images, and smells and locked them inside my mind, affecting my mood and influence. There are times when friends or family members will ask me to share some of my dark moments from work, but I

usually ignore them and leave those memories locked inside my head. But if they only knew what I knew.

Over time, I discovered that working in law enforcement created undue stress, which caused me to have a short temper. The lack of sleep, long hours, isolation from society, and constant exposure to harmful human elements made everything feel even worse. Being in constant danger, you cannot help but become suspicious of everything and everyone around you.

Over time, I found that you cannot just sit still and do nothing, not even while off duty and at home. I often attempted to find a hobby or some activity to keep my mind active, which may have helped my mental stability. Sometimes, when I see a particular interest, I try to find another agent or friend with whom I can influence and share in the fun.

One significant aspect was that people in law enforcement develop a fraternal relationship that can become extraordinarily strong. Whether during the line of duty or a personal crisis, your law enforcement family will be there for you, come hell or high water.

I can tell you that in law enforcement, no day is the same. I appreciated that no two calls were alike, and I never knew what or where I would be sent. I admit that it was often overly exciting, and to add to that, your ability to help people daily was very fulfilling.

I always enjoyed the camaraderie among my peers, which often deflected negative work thoughts. It usually helped to talk with individuals who were going through the same issues. But it was all a balancing act because whenever I got the good, I knew I would also get the bad.

At the time I decided to retire, I saw that it was not an enjoyable time to be in law enforcement in an era of police ambushes and active shooters. I could see that this country was occupied by many naïve bleeding hearts who seemed to blame the police, who had done nothing wrong, and set free the criminals who had committed crimes. I could not understand how anyone would want to be a police officer these days and put up with so much nonsense (crap) from the public. Some law enforcement officers would rather appease the public over any issue, leaving themselves vulnerable. After working in law enforcement for forty-six years, I am deeply proud when I look in the mirror. I feel a thrill and triumph after a successful lifesaving effort or the arrest of a dangerous criminal.

Throughout my years in law enforcement, I gained valuable insights. I worked with many officers and agents, observing their enforcement style, and I even had the opportunity to train other officers and agents.

I remember working night shifts, which was great until things slowed down. When it got to be five or six a.m., then it

started to suck. I learned that when you go to a domestic disturbance call, you have to be careful because the family members will attack you when you handcuff their loved one who has assaulted the family. It happens so often that you start to expect it.

Preparing reports directly reflects who you are and how you perform your work. Incomplete or sloppy report writing will haunt you for years to come.

One of the most important lessons I learned is that the most rigid, strongest police officers can lose it in a death investigation involving a baby or child. I know this for a fact.

While working with the BRPD one rainy night, an accident occurred on the interstate near the Sherwood Forest Boulevard exit. Numerous cars were involved, and many injuries occurred when people were thrown from their vehicles.

When I arrived, I was informed that a tiny female baby had been thrown from the car and couldn't be found. I immediately began to search for the baby along with everyone else, and as I walked down in the ditch area where there were pretty high weeds, I accidentally stepped on the baby lying on the ground. I picked her up and held her tight in my arms while checking for life, but she was gone. I remembered holding her cuddled in my arms, telling her many times how sorry I was for stepping on her.

You're not human if you don't believe it will affect you. Incidents like this stay with you for the rest of your life, and now and then, something will occur that makes me think about that night. Maybe, one day, when I'm in heaven, I will see her happy and playing with other children.

While many things have changed over the years, most law enforcement officers' passion for protecting their communities is constant. Whether serving 20 years ago or just retiring, most officers display courage, compassion, and bravery.

As a profession, we must maintain a healthy lifestyle that demands an ethic of professional service. We must also require a restoration of our rightful place as community guardians. To the extent that we can counter false and negative portrayals, we can question what has become the overall public belief and restore the respect that police have never stopped earning. Although I am now retired, I deeply admire the job and wish all newcomers luck for a healthy and successful career.

CHAPTER 5

Applying for Federal Law Enforcement

After serving for over nine years with the BRPD, I decided to expand my horizons and seek employment with the federal government. I applied with the U.S. Border Patrol (USBP) and the U.S. Marshals Service because, at the time, those were the only two agencies hiring. Both agencies were willing to substitute the seventeen semester hours I had left to complete my college degree for my law enforcement experience.

Working in federal law enforcement will provide me with high job security. I knew federal law enforcement agencies had field offices nationwide and in other countries. These locations would allow me to choose where to work and possibly switch locations.

Luckily, I received a letter from the USBP explaining that I must first take the written examination. I signed up and took the exam at a library in Baton Rouge, and I passed with a high enough score to proceed to the next step. I was later scheduled for several extensive oral interviews at the U.S. Border Patrol Sector in New Orleans. After passing the interviews, I had to undergo a thorough background investigation and then pass a physical and mental examination. But unbelievably, I passed everything!

I later received a message from the U.S. Marshals Service about employment, but I had already started the process with USBP and was well on my way to being hired. I didn't want to do anything that might jeopardize that process, so I declined the U.S. Marshal's proposal.

I conducted extensive research and weighed the pros and cons of both agencies, ultimately deciding to work with the USBP. Mainly because the agents maintain the safety and security of the United States' borders with Canada and Mexico. I also read that the USBP agents served on the front line for

the now U.S. Customs and Border Protection (CBP) within the Department of Homeland Security (DHS). Remember that when I was hired in 1988, the U.S. Border Patrol (USBP) was under the authority of the U.S. Immigration and Naturalization Service (INS), which was part of the U.S. Department of

Justice (DOJ).

What is a U.S. Border Patrol Agent

As a USBP agent, you are responsible for monitoring and protecting over 8,000 miles of international borders to make sure undocumented immigrants, drugs, and goods do not come into the country. Working on the border, you identify and prevent human trafficking and narcotic contraband while working alongside other local and state law enforcement agencies.

A more specific duty would be to screen people entering and leaving the United States, seize illegal shipments, prevent the entry of terrorist-type weapons, and conduct surveillance along the border. I knew the work could be dangerous and that I would be required to work many nighttime hours.

Working with the USBP, I would be introduced to national intelligence networks, collaborate with local law enforcement groups, and utilize military and police technologies.

The USBP was offering me many new opportunities regarding law enforcement techniques, and I would be introduced to a different world of law enforcement. I had

never seen the technologies and equipment to which I would be introduced, so this would be a completely new concept for me to learn and become familiar with. This new aspect of law enforcement would be a challenge for me, and I wanted to learn everything.

After completing the hiring process, I was informed I would be stationed in Marfa, Texas, as my first duty assignment. Before attending the academy, the notice also stated that I must visit the Marfa Sector first to complete the necessary Human Resources paperwork for employment. This would also allow you to see where you will be working and the living environment.

So, after accepting my notice of employment, I was given a date to report to Marfa to spend one week processing employment paperwork before attending the academy.

Off to Marfa!

CHAPTER 6

First to Marfa, Texas

As stated in the previous chapter, after getting through the hiring process and accepting the employment offer from USBP, I was informed that I would be stationed in Marfa, Texas, as my duty assignment. I was told that before attending the academy, I had first to visit the Marfa Sector to complete the necessary Human Resources paperwork for employment and to determine where I would be living and working. After a week of orientation in Marfa, I would be sent to the academy to complete the twenty weeks of training in the Border Patrol Academy.

I began to get everything together, preparing for my departure to Marfa. Linda and I worked closely together, coordinating everything because I would be away for three months studying at the academy. I had great excitement building up and was looking forward to getting things started. I had never been to Marfa, so I looked it up on the map and researched the town and the surrounding area.

It all sounded and looked exciting, but a part of me was dealing with the fact that I was going out there by myself, leaving Linda and Jacob in Amite. So, I was excited and scared at the same time. Also, it was the unknown that played with my head, too. It wasn't just about relocating my family to Marfa; it was also about me changing jobs. I would no longer be a police officer and move into a new role as a Border Patrol Agent working for the federal government. I had to take it one day at a time.

I was leaving my job as a police officer with BRPD, leaving Amite, leaving Linda and Jacob, and heading somewhere I had never been before, all while checking in on a new job. That was a lot to take in at once. But I kept telling myself I was not the only person doing this because others would be out there with me, coming in from around the country.

I haven't met them yet, but I will when I check in at Marfa Sector. Then, when I arrive at the academy, people from around the country will check in to attend my class. I sucked it up and put my big boy pants on, and prepared myself. I was determined to give it my best shot.

On August 20, 1988, I flew from the Baton Rouge airport to El Paso, Texas. I grabbed a cab from the airport to the Greyhound bus station. From there, I would take a Greyhound bus to Marfa. I remembered the flight to El Paso and Marfa as if it had happened yesterday.

When I arrived at the bus station in El Paso, I sat in the terminal, looking around at the diversity of people walking around me. People were sitting in their seats holding dogs; several had small boxes containing real live chickens. The entire waiting area inside the terminal "stunk" with the smell of animals. The scent did not bother anyone too much because several women were making sandwiches for their children to eat, and one man sitting a few chairs from me was eating something that smelled bad, but it looked like a burrito.

While waiting for my bus, I was starving for something to eat. I didn't think I had enough time to go anywhere and find anything because the bus to Marfa was expected to arrive at any moment. I was determined not to miss that bus, as I would not want to be stuck in El Paso overnight, sleeping at the terminal.

I looked around for a vending machine, and the one I saw was just about empty. As I looked for another vending machine, the bus arrived at the terminal. I returned to my seat in the terminal, but someone was now sitting there. I stood and paced, waiting to board the bus because I was ready to go. I had had enough of the bus terminal and was prepared to get to Marfa—at least, I thought I was.

Finally, the announcement was made for everyone going to Marfa to line up for boarding. When that announcement was made, everyone sitting with me in the lobby rushed outside to the bus. I stood there thinking, "Why the hurry?" I had a ticket in my hand and knew I would be getting on, so I saw no reason to rush.

I walked outside and took my place in line to board the bus. When I finally approached the bus, I discovered why everyone rushed to get on first. I quickly learned that you do not want to sit in the back of the bus, where the restroom is located. That was why everyone rushed; they had done this before and knew how to avoid the back seats.

Luckily, I sat in a seat in the middle of the bus next to an elderly Hispanic lady who was holding a large paper bag in her lap. From what I could see, the bag was filled with assorted vegetables, and she had that bag in her lap for hours until she got off the bus at one of the stops. She was a lovely lady who did not speak English but smiled a lot at me. Besides, I was not in the mood to talk with anyone because I was tired, everything stunk severely, and I was starving. I just wanted to sleep for a while on the bus.

It was around 8:00 p.m. when the Greyhound departed from the El Paso station, and I recall that bus ride as if it had happened just last night. Traveling to Marfa, we made many stops in small towns, and at every stop, some people got off, and more got on. The driver announced a ten-minute stop at each location for us to step off and stretch our legs. If you want to get something to eat in the store, you'd better be back on time. There was always a small store where the bus stopped at each location, and although I don't remember the town, I recall getting off and grabbing a soft drink and a honey bun. I was too worried to eat anything heavy for fear of getting sick or having to use the bathroom while on the bus.

With all the scheduled stops, the chickens cackling, and assorted pets on the bus, it was extremely hard to rest. As I looked around the bus, I saw many people had no problem napping. They were used to traveling that way, and the smell and noise did not affect them.

Finally, at 1:00 a.m. on August 21st, we arrived in Marfa after a five-hour bus ride. Several days prior, I had contacted the Marfa Sector and requested that an agent pick me up at the bus station upon my arrival. Fortunately, an agent awaited me when I got off the bus. After retrieving my luggage, the agent informed me that he had been assigned to work at the Marfa checkpoint outside of town that night and was instructed to meet me. I was so glad to see him standing there when I arrived because I knew the hotel was about a quarter mile from the bus station, and at that time of the morning, it would have been a hell of a walk for me.

I worried so much while riding on the bus, even praying that someone would be able to meet me when I arrived. So, when I saw that agent standing there, it was a huge relief, and my prayers were answered.

I had reservations at the Thunderbird Hotel in Marfa, the only hotel in town. The agent drove me there and dropped me off at the front door, saying he had to return to the checkpoint and wishing me luck.

A phone number on the hotel's front door was posted, stating that I needed to call to arrange for someone to check me in. There was a pay phone outside, so I called the number and waited about fifteen minutes until a vehicle pulled up to the hotel. An elderly lady exited the car and escorted me inside so I could check in and obtain my room key. She told me she worked at the front desk, but it closed at midnight, and she didn't live on the premises. She told me she was aware of my arrival and left a note for me. She said she lived about 10 minutes away and awaited my call. She was a lovely lady, and we had several enjoyable conversations about Marfa, the Border Patrol, and many other topics related to the businesses around town. She was helpful, and I relied on her during my stay.

I checked in, received my room key around 1:30 a.m., and walked to my room, which was located across the parking lot.

I went into my room, unpacked, and showered before bed. The flight and bus ride experience, having someone meet me, and calling to get someone back to the hotel to check me in had completely exhausted me. I was stressed out to the max, and to say I was tired was an understatement. Even lying in bed, I took many deep breaths to calm down and fall asleep. I planned to stay at the Thunderbird during my visit to Marfa that week.

I awoke around 8:00 a.m. that Sunday and couldn't wait to get dressed and explore the town. I finally left my room and walked around Marfa, taking everything in. I walked for quite a while, observing and trying to make sense of everything I saw. I started questioning myself about what I had gotten myself into, and it wasn't long before I wanted to convince myself that everything would be ok and that I had done the right thing coming out to Marfa.

Honestly, my first impression of Marfa was not a good one. At the time, Marfa appeared as a ghost town that Sunday morning. I walked around for several hours, trying to take it all in, but I felt secluded from the world I once knew. I came from civilization and thought I had seen everything imaginable, yet I stood in a "new world" that was hard to comprehend. I felt like I was in one of those towns in a Western movie, with people walking around and no one speaking English.

Since it was a Sunday, all the stores were closed, so I could only walk and look. But I found a café on the main street going through town. I went inside and sat in a booth, starving. When the server came, I ordered two breakfast burritos with everything, along with a glass of milk to drink. I was hungry, so I ordered two burritos. The server looked at me and questioned the two burritos I had ordered. She spoke decent English, so I knew she understood me. I said yes because I was very hungry and ready to eat. She looked at me and said, "Coming up."

About ten minutes later, the server brought two separate plates and set them before me. Each plate contained a massive burrito filled with everything inside, covered in a green sauce, and topped with lettuce, tomatoes, and a generous amount of peppers. It also had rice and beans beside it. I didn't realize when I ordered that it came as a plate-type meal with all the food.

Anyway, I was hungry, so I tore into the food, finishing off the first plate and most of the second, but I took the rest to eat later. I was on a budget and saved wherever I could. I remember the food being good and tasty.

It was around noon when I finished my breakfast, so I returned to the Thunderbird. Walking into my room, I fell on the bed with a full belly and was still tired. I couldn't believe I left a respectable job and family to come to this Wild West. I considered returning to that environment where I felt safe; I knew the people and my surroundings. But something inside me kept saying to give it a chance and wait to see where this would go. Besides, I haven't even made it to my first day of work to see what that would be like. I knew civilization had to be out there in Marfa, but where?

In Marfa, Spanish was the predominant language, and at the time, I didn't understand enough Spanish to know what anyone was trying to say to me. The server in the café spoke English, which was a good thing. I discovered later that most of the agents working in Marfa spoke Spanish. For the rest of the day, I stayed in my room, thinking and contemplating what I had done, trying to make sense of everything.

Report to Marfa Sector

On Monday morning, August 22, 1988, at 8:00 a.m., I reported to the Marfa Border Patrol Sector for a week of orientation, meetings with the Chief Patrol Agent, and completing paperwork before attending the academy. The Human Resources Department paperwork was prepared and ready for my signature. Additionally, visiting the location gave me a sense of what it would be like to live and work there after graduating from the academy. Now, if you didn't like it there or decided this was not for you, it was time to resign before they spent too much money on you.

That morning, I walked to the Marfa Sector, which wasn't far from the hotel. I noticed a fence with a locked, secured gate at the front entrance surrounding the sector. I pressed the call button on the front gate, and a lady came over to the intercom and said she wouldn't let me in. I explained to her who I was and that I was supposed to start work that day. After a few minutes, I heard her and others laughing over the intercom, and she finally opened the gate to let me enter.

When I approached the main building entrance door, it started again. When I pushed the call button to be let in, I heard over the intercom, "Who is it?" Everyone there was full of pranks for the new guys coming in. Luckily, five other new agents showed up that day, which took a little pressure off of me.

Along with the other new agents, I spent the day watching a film, completing paperwork, and undergoing basic orientation.

It was a long day because you had to take everything in while learning names, ranks, and who was present in the office.

After getting off work that day, I learned that the other new agents were staying at the same hotel, and we all walked back together. I went to my room and relaxed while lying on my bed. A few minutes later, there was a knock at my door, and several of the BP agents from Marfa came by to bring beer. We gathered the other new agents, talked, and drank a few beers. We laughed a lot and talked about where we came from, etc., and the agents explained that as soon as we graduated from the academy, we could work and become part of the group there. That made me feel more at ease, as if I were starting to blend in with the others. As it turned out, everyone there was friendly, which helped me get settled in and feel more comfortable.

The following day, everything got more serious with our training regarding the job's entails and duties. I first learned about the checkpoint outside town and even observed the procedures. We stopped a few cars at the checkpoint, and I observed the ensuing interaction.

The agents showed me what sign-cutting was all about, and we went out into the desert to practice. I didn't do too badly for my first time tracking footprints. I was also taught where to look for water if I ever needed it. Water was always located on the numerous ranches in the area that had windmills and vats underneath them.

I attended training daily until I left for the academy. It was a productive week, and I learned a great deal.

At the end of the week, on Saturday, all of us new agents were taken to Odessa, Texas, to pick up another new agent who had checked in at his station. We were then taken to El Paso to board a flight to Jacksonville, Florida.

After arriving in Jacksonville, a Federal Law Enforcement Training Center (FLETC) bus was waiting to transport us to the academy.

That was a long day, too! On to the academy.

Chapter 7

U.S. Border Patrol Academy

After my week in Marfa, where I completed all the human resource paperwork and attended orientation days, I was ready to attend the academy at the Federal Law Enforcement Training Center (FLETC) in Glynco, GA. By now, I knew what I was getting into and was looking forward to the academy and getting back to work in Marfa.

In the sector, I met people from all over the U.S. who were there for government work, just like me. I listened to their stories of how they got there and what they went through, and I could relate to them. We shared funny stories of our travels to Marfa, and I stopped feeling sorry for myself and started to see a future ahead. Despite its remote location, I made friends during the week and began to enjoy it.

Beginning a new job was exciting yet intimidating. While this new job presented opportunities for growth, learning, and career advancement, the transition brought me a significant amount of stress, anxiety, and uncertainty. The pressure to perform, adapt to a new environment, and build new relationships with colleagues weighed heavily on my mental state.

After leaving Marfa and traveling to the academy, I was accompanied by many emotions; the anticipation of starting the academy and getting a new job brought a sense of excitement. I thought about the new possibilities, learning experiences, and the chance to meet new people, which motivated and enthused me. But underneath my excitement, I felt anxious about fitting in, meeting expectations, and proving myself in a new position. It was dealing with the uncertainties about my new position and attending the academy, but I knew I could adapt to any situation.

My first thoughts about this new position were overwhelming. Attempting to learn a new system, experiencing a different workplace culture, and trying to absorb a great amount of information in the academy could lead to cognitive overload for me. I knew this, and I started preparing myself for a mental overload.

Border Patrol Academy

From Marfa, we flew to Jacksonville, Florida, then hopped onto a bus waiting to transport us to FLETC. I got off the bus at FLETC and reported to the academy office, where I was given an orientation package, a map of the facility, and a diagram indicating the location of the chow line. I was also given my dorm number, where I would reside for three months. I was assigned to Border Patrol Class #225 and received information on which building to report to for class assignments and to meet the head instructor the following morning.

I recall wearing the uniform the following day and finding my way to the dining hall for breakfast. The food was terrific, and you could order what you wanted or pick from anything and everything on the carts. After breakfast, I walked over to the building where my assigned class was to meet and where I met my new classmates. We all stood around talking and waiting for someone to tell us what we needed to do. We waited until 8:00 a.m., as previously instructed.

We noticed other classes forming up at attention and getting in straight lines, just like the military formation. They seemed organized and looked like they had been doing it for a while, as they appeared to be doing it well, whatever they were doing. It is approaching 8:10 a.m., and no instructor has arrived to guide us or inform us of our next steps.

I had befriended an ex-military male classmate and asked him exactly what the other classes were doing. He explained that it appeared they were forming a military-style formation and preparing for an inspection by their instructors. I suggested we try to do the same, so he and I got everyone together and attempted to mirror the other classes. We divided our class into two groups, as the others had done. I took half of the group, and he took the other half. We lined up just as the other groups had done, and fortunately, our fellow classmates listened to us and fell into line as we asked. I stood out in front of my group, and as I lined everyone up, my friend was doing the same with his group.

Once we formed, all the other groups began marching off the lot in different directions. We didn't know what to do, so we stood there in formation, waiting patiently.

Our classmates started asking questions, wanting to know what to do, but at that time, four USBP academy instructors walked out of the building and over to where we were standing. They walked straight to me and my friend and told us congratulations, you two, or the squad leaders. The class was now known as Class 225, groups A and B. I was assigned to lead Group A for the duration of the academy. The instructors informed us that they had been watching us and waiting to see who among the new trainees was willing to step up and take charge.

The academy curriculum comprised 940 hours of class instruction in physical fitness, immigration and naturalization law, basic law, firearms training, and driving techniques. The classes included simulations in which Border Patrol instructors and contracted role players (paid actors) acted out various possible real-life scenarios, including stopping armed drug smugglers, detaining individuals crossing the border illegally, and conducting traffic stops.

The Academy was a rigorous training program that prepared you for the challenges of working and protecting the nation's borders.

While in the academy, I spent a sizable portion of my curriculum learning Spanish to communicate with individuals along the border. We learned basic questions to process the illegals we apprehended along the border.

Firearms training at the academy was critical. After completing all the training, I had to pass a series of qualifications to demonstrate my competency with a weapon before I could graduate from the academy and be issued a service weapon.

Arriving at the academy, I questioned my competence, feeling that I wasn't qualified to be there. My self-doubt negatively impacted my confidence and mental well-being. Many people told me when I arrived that adapting to a new workflow, setting expectations, and adjusting to the social environment would take time.

So, after I arrived and settled into my room, the first step was convincing myself to be patient with everything. I needed to take the time to acclimate to the campus and what was before me. Like everyone else, I met with the counselor at the academy to get advice on how to adjust appropriately without being confused.

The counselor gave us valuable advice. First, she recommended that we acknowledge and recognize our emotions. Feeling excited, anxious, and unsure about things was normal. She also suggested that we journal our daily activities at the end of each day.

She told us to understand that it's okay to take time to adjust and to set realistic goals for our first few weeks. Instead of striving for perfection, we should focus on learning, forming meaningful relationships, and adapting to our new environment. Then, we should reflect on our experience and acknowledge each achievement, no matter how small.

The counselor's advice was very helpful. I often had to stop and tell myself I was where I was and doing what I was doing. Each day was new, and I accepted it for what it was.

FLETC

When I attended the Border Patrol Academy at the Federal Law Enforcement Training Center (FLETC) in 1988, the entire facility was operated under the Department of Treasury. In March 2003, it was turned over to be managed by the newly formed Department of Homeland Security (DHS). DHS now operates the most prominent school in the country for police officers, detectives, Secret Service agents, Border Patrol agents, and other federal law enforcement professionals. FLETC is where law enforcement professionals learn how to protect and defend our communities from criminals and terrorists. FLETC is located in Glynco, GA., next to Brunswick, GA.

I have returned to FLETC several times since graduating from the academy and have been amazed at how much it has grown. Whenever I returned for training, I saw new classroom buildings and dormitories constructed everywhere. Remember that the entire campus was like a massive university with training for all federal, state, and local agencies. You can look up FLETC online and read all about the facility.

Upon graduating, I was issued a Smith & Wesson Model 66

.357 Magnum as my service weapon to take into the field. I liked that weapon because it was easy to use and manage. With that weapon, I shot a consistent score of 295 and above out of a possible three hundred score. I completed the twenty weeks of training at the academy, which also included completing the following courses:

Nationality Law, Immigration Law, and Applied Authority: Learning to recognize violations of federal criminal statutes and either take appropriate action or refer the matter to another federal agency of authority.

Physical Techniques Program—This training will get you in shape to an acceptable standard that will enable you to perform the day-to-day duties of an agent working in the field environment. Then came the driver training course, designed to teach you the safe and efficient operation of a motor vehicle. We drove cars around obstacle courses and participated in high-speed driving.

The USBP academy was brutal—the most demanding training I ever attended. It was a lot more strenuous than the BRPD academy. Still, what helped me the most was my experience attending the six-week Police Officer Standard of Training (POST) training at LSU, followed by the BRPD academy training and all my other law enforcement classes. All this training combined helped me tremendously in getting through the academy.

I know one thing for sure: the day I left the academy, a load was lifted off my shoulders because I had already done enough marching, studying, reading, physical techniques, and firearms training. I shot so much that I got calluses on my trigger finger. I was tired of the pressure of being everywhere and on time.

Linda and Jacob attended my graduation, and we prepared for our journey to Marfa. It was exciting because we were headed to West Texas alone and had no one to lean on. I said it was exciting, but it was scary, too.

Moving from Amite PD to BRPD was a strain, but now I'm taking my family out west. Linda and Jacob had not been to Marfa before, so this would be a new experience.

Although I knew what I was getting into, they didn't, and that scared me the most. I was doing my best to stay upbeat and remain positive for them, as I remembered how I had first arrived and seen Marfa, so I didn't know how they would feel upon first sight.

I prayed for the best because I had so much riding on this move and my new job. One of the first things I did when we arrived in Marfa was to check into the Little League Baseball program. When I learned that there was one, I was a happy camper. I knew I could get Jacob involved in baseball, occupying his mind and time and taking some stress away.

Linda was a different story. She would have to make many sacrifices regarding everything she was accustomed to doing and having. She, too, was leaving friends, family, and the comfortable environment of Amite to accompany me to an unknown destination.

Today, I look back on these decisions with mixed feelings. Of course, I'm glad we did it because it helped us grow as a family, and we learned to rely on each other. Plus, we would not be where we are today if we hadn't ventured off and experienced Marfa. If I had to do things all over again, I would still make the same decision to go to Marfa, but I would approach it differently and take advantage of what Marfa has to offer. Not just the town or the work but the entire countryside. We didn't take advantage of our surroundings, which included the surrounding mountains, deserts, and the Marfa Lights.

I often put Linda and Jacob through a lot by asking them to pick up our belongings and move to West Texas for my job. I'm proud they trusted and loved me and followed me out there. I don't know where I would be or what I would have done if they had said "no." I hope they understand that everything I did was for the betterment of our family. Of course, I wanted to continue a career in federal law enforcement, and I was willing to do what it took to achieve that goal. However, I am grateful that Linda trusted me and had faith in what I was doing. This is one of a thousand reasons I love her even more now.

Jacob probably felt like a dog on a leash being led around, but he wasn't. He was a trooper who did his best in any situation to help us remain a family. I love you, Son!

I learned that relocating for work can be exciting and challenging, especially when it involves Linda and Jacob. We had to balance my career ambitions and their needs, which took thoughtful planning and execution. While planning our move, I had to ensure a smooth transition for everyone involved. This was a significant life change for all of us, and I wanted it to be manageable and rewarding.

One of the first steps I took was to communicate openly with Linda. I shared details about my new job, the move, and what she should expect. Her understanding of my reasons for relocating and how it would benefit us created some excitement and helped reduce some anxiety. Linda could ask questions and express her feelings about leaving behind friends and familiar surroundings. I included Linda and Jacob in all discussions as much as possible, which I hoped made them feel somewhat engaged in the moving process. This

wasn't all about me; they had a say and were allowed their input.

We even created a timeline together, including packing days and moving dates, hopefully giving Linda some control. I also did my best, as did Linda, to reassure Jacob that his input was important, too, and everything would be fine.

Now, let's go back to Marfa!

Chapter 8

Marfa, Texas Border Patrol Sector

After graduating from the academy on January 2, 1989, we left FLETC and traveled back to Amite to pack and load our belongings to prepare for our move to Marfa. I had approximately a week to get things together and return to Marfa for work. We had our house for sale in Amite, which we had purchased several years prior and hoped to sell soon.

After a few days of packing and planning in Amite, we loaded our belongings and prepared for the trip to Marfa. We said goodbye to friends in Amite and took off for Marfa.

Moving to another state was a time-consuming process that required patience and planning, from packing our belongings to finding a place to live.

When we arrived in Marfa, I had arranged for us to rent a small house near the sector's office. We moved in with our belongings, and Linda immediately started making us a home. After moving in, all we had to do was learn about our new community, which was essential for us to settle in smoothly.

We explored neighborhoods, schools, recreational activities, and cultural opportunities. We started identifying areas aligned with our lifestyle and found places to visit where we felt at home. We immediately attempted to connect with people in our community who helped ease the transition for us and Jacob.

Adjusting to our new environment took some time, but we established a routine with my new work schedule and felt more secure. This included setting my work schedules, figuring out routes for school and work, and Linda finding the local grocery stores, doctor's offices, and other essential services.

Linda had no problem exploring our new surroundings, making new friends, and getting involved in the community.

As I stated, the Border Patrol was the uniformed law enforcement arm of the then Department of Justice (DOJ) and is now under the Department of Homeland Security (DHS) jurisdiction.

Marfa was not a bad place to live and work. It was on top of a mountain with wide-open spaces, hot summers, and cold winters. My first winter in Marfa was cold, and it snowed several inches that winter. I never thought I would see snow in Marfa, but it becomes understandable considering its location on the mountain.

Immigration Checkpoint

After reporting to the Marfa Sector, my first assignment was working at the vehicle checkpoint. The Marfa checkpoint was stationary, with a small mobile trailer on the side of the highway connecting Marfa to the Mexican border in Presidio, Texas. The checkpoint was approximately three miles south of Marfa, so vehicle traffic traveling north from Presidio to Marfa came to it. Reaching the checkpoint, vehicles had to pull over and speak with a Border Patrol agent.

The Border Patrol checkpoints are inspection stations between 25 and 100 miles inland from the U.S.-Mexico and U.S.-Canada borders. They serve to deter illegal immigration and smuggling activities.

(Marfa Checkpoint)

Working at the checkpoint was not difficult, given my background as a narcotics agent with the Baton Rouge Police Department. As I worked on the point, I observed the drivers' body language, nervous behavior, and reactions to my questions when a vehicle approached the checkpoint. Additionally, I could quickly determine if any vehicle modifications or alterations had been made. If something on the vehicle were altered, such as a fender or lights, I would notice it quickly. I also knew that drug smugglers would do this to conceal their drugs in those areas, and when they replace that part on the vehicle, you can see the disturbance where it was taken off. Usually, they would use either new screws or some newer material that, when completed, would look out of place for the kind of vehicle.

On occasion, we also used a narcotic drug K-9 around the vehicle, and those dogs were about 99% accurate when they alerted on a vehicle.

One fun aspect of working at the checkpoint was disassembling vehicles to locate hidden drugs. We tore many vehicles apart at the checkpoint because people wouldn't cooperate and tell us where the drugs were located, so we took the vehicle apart until we found what we were looking for.

We knew that the drugs were hidden because sometimes you can smell them yourself, a drug dog would hit the vehicle, or you can tell where the car was modified in some form that may be hiding narcotics. Usually, when we took apart the rear taillight, you can see drugs stuffed inside, or when you check the fuel tanks. Rarely did any real drug smuggler cooperate with us.

On occasion, trucks would have two fuel tanks installed, one for fuel and the other full of narcotics. This trick didn't work well for the smuggler, and the technique didn't last long. Dealers began to think that having two tanks on their vehicles would lead to them being searched.

I could type for days explaining the different encounters we experienced at the checkpoint. The checkpoint was a fun place to work because the drugs came to you, and you did not have to go out to search for them. It was unbelievable how so many people carried and traveled with drugs while that close to the Mexican border.

Sign Cutting

I learned how to sign cut while in Marfa, which was actual physical evidence of the environment left behind by humans. I learned that a person cannot walk on the ground without leaving a visible sign, such as a footprint or environmental disturbance. We were trying to find and track this sign in the dirt. While sign-cutting, we traveled up into the mountains and down to the border, passing through some beautiful countryside.

Many times, on my days off, Linda, Jacob, and I would take trips to the mountains to sightsee and take in the beauty of the countryside.

When most people think of tracking, they usually think of following footprints, but when you are tracking, you are looking for much more. You look for kicked-over rocks, soil depressions, clothing fibers, and any changes in that particular environment. You are looking for any disturbance left behind by the person or persons being tracked.

All agents in Marfa utilize sign cutting, which remains one of the most effective tools for locating people and gathering intelligence information regarding drug and human smuggling.

Ground Sensors

The Marfa Sector also utilized sensors planted in the ground and cameras concealed in various locations within the desert and mountains. These sensors were placed on previous routes that smugglers had taken or potential future routes. Someone walking on or near the sensor would alert the Border Patrol Sector. When this occurred, an agent would be dispatched to that location to determine who or what had triggered the sensor. Occasionally, it could have been an animal walking by or stepping on the sensor. When you get to the location, you can see tracks of either animals or human footprints.

Working at the checkpoint, responding to sensors, and patrolling in Marfa was a terrific learning experience. I gained a profound understanding of immigration law and border law enforcement. The amount of knowledge I received opened my eyes to what the Border Patrol was attempting to do to prevent illegal entry into the United States.

My brief time in Marfa was a lot of fun, not only at work but also exploring the countryside and driving up in the mountains with Linda, Jacob, and me. We rode down to the Rio Grande River, which was an experience. Seeing the river and working while catching illegals sneaking across was as exciting as possible.

On my day off, we took scenic drives to visit the Chinati Hot Springs in Marfa, TX, near the Chihuahuan Desert. Sometimes, we would watch the Marfa Ghost Lights outside town at night. Jacob had plenty of good times playing baseball with his friends from Marfa and all the Mexican friends he made.

I never really got too involved with Jacob and his elementary school. Linda took care of that because I was so

busy learning a new job and all the procedures that came with it.

We have many photos of Jacob playing baseball in Marfa, where he also made many friends from Marfa, Presidio, and Mexico.

(Below is the Rio Grande River at Presidio, TX)

Many of our baseball games were held in Presidio on the border.

Presidio. Before the games started, we waited for some Mexican kids to cross the Rio Grande and come up to the baseball field. Back then, living was so much easier than it is today. The Mexican kids would walk across the shallow part of the river and come to practice baseball or play games with us. Even their parents would walk across the river with their lawn chairs and sometimes bring their small barbeque pits to cook.

No one worries about crossing through the Presidio port of entry on game day or even during practice. Everyone knew they would walk back across the border via the Rio Grande when the game or practice was over. As I said, times were simple, and there was trust, but that's no longer true.

Linda and I made many new friends while living in Marfa, including other border patrol families and Hispanic families. We later learned that most people there spoke English, allowing us to communicate effectively with them. For our cat Sam, this was her first stop during my career living outside Louisiana, and she was now a Texas cat. One day, Sam decided to walk outside the house and tour the area alone.

(Right is Jacob and a friend)

Later that day, we started to miss her and couldn't find her anywhere. We still could not see her when it got dark outside, so we decided to go to bed. The following day, Sam was outside the door waiting on the porch to come inside the house. She gave us a real scare that night because she had never gone missing before or even been outside overnight. I guess she wanted to explore for herself, but she never did it again.

As Border Patrol Agents, we shot assorted weapons all the time, even when we were out in the desert patrolling. It would take nothing for us to pull the vehicle over on the side of the road and take out our MP5s (9mm), revolvers, and shotguns to shoot at anything for target practice. Firing one's weapon for target practice was common in a remote desert.

Rent House

While in Marfa, we lived in two different rental houses. When I first left the academy, I stayed in a small place similar to a mother-in-law suite that another agent owned. It had two small bedrooms and a bathroom. A friend stationed in Marfa and attending my academy class shared the apartment with me. Later, after graduation, I brought Linda and Jacob out with me and found a little house to rent in town. After we moved in and lived there for a while, we discovered that it was a little small for us and our furniture.

In April 1989, we decided to look for a larger house to rent, and it didn't take long before we found one located around the corner from our current residence. It had plenty of room, and we could spread out and live comfortably. We paid $125 monthly at our first rental house, but as I mentioned, it was too small for our comfort. We paid $175 monthly for rent in the larger house we moved to. We considered those prices high rent, but we knew we needed the extra space, so we paid the extra rent was not an option.

After spending a year in Marfa, I had an opportunity to pursue other ventures and expand my knowledge while learning a new

position. A position became available in Minneapolis, MN., for an Immigration Inspector at the Minneapolis-St. Paul International Airport.

Our first house is on the left and our second is on the right. Honestly, I knew nothing about being an Immigration Inspector, but from what I remembered about the Immigration Inspectors working in Presidio, they were earning way more money than I was. I, at least, knew that.

As usual, I researched and learned that Immigration Inspectors fall under the U.S. Immigration and Naturalization Service, just like the U.S. Border Patrol. Additionally, Immigration Inspectors worked considerable overtime and were paid double time for working on Sundays. Upon reviewing the position descriptions, I noticed that Immigration Inspectors performed the same duties I was performing, except they carried out their responsibilities at a port of entry (POE).

The way I saw it, I was out chasing illegals and inspecting people at a checkpoint while Inspectors were at a

POE, and the people were coming to them. The picture above is after considering it and speaking with Linda, I decided to try it. I submitted the necessary transfer paperwork for the position. Besides, it sounded intriguing to live and work in Minneapolis.

It wasn't long after submitting my paperwork that I was officially offered the position.

On July 2, 1989, I accepted the position of Immigration Inspector at the Minneapolis-St. Paul International Airport. I learned that transfers don't move fast. Paperwork with the government is slow, and nothing moves too quickly.

I also learned that having a clear strategy when relocating as a family for work was crucial to our success. I did my best to align our expectations, and understanding how the move impacted each of us helped me create a plan that met all our needs. For example, I tried to choose a house close to my workplace, which reduced my commute time, allowing me more time with Linda and Jacob for family activities. Likewise, Linda was involved in most of the decision-making about schools for Jacob and how we developed our friends. This included meeting with neighbors and coworkers and attending community events. We participated in local activities, such as baseball for Jacob, which helped us connect more with the community.

After receiving my transfer orders, we packed up and headed North to Minneapolis.

Chapter 9

MINNEAPOLIS - St. PAUL

On July 2, 1989, I became a U.S. Immigration Inspector in Minneapolis, part of the inspection program. In 1989, the inspection program fell under the directive of the U.S. Immigration & Naturalization Service, Department of Justice. Today, it falls under the U.S. Customs and Border Protection, a department of the U.S. Department of Homeland Security.

Upon our arrival in Minneapolis, we checked into a hotel and then started mapping out a game plan for where we wanted to live. We researched and found a real estate company that assisted renters with finding apartments or houses to rent. We went there, and while we waited in the lobby area to speak with someone, we overheard other people discussing apartment prices with the staff. The prices they were discussing for an apartment sounded ridiculous to us, and some prices for apartments were higher than the mortgage on our home in Amite. We had no plans of getting one of those pricey apartments, but instead, we stayed within the price range we were accustomed to. I recalled that the prices of apartments in Baton Rouge averaged $150 – $300 a month, so I was looking to pay in that price range.

When it came our turn to speak with a staff member, we explained our situation and that we were looking for a two-bedroom apartment. We also told her the price range we were prepared to pay. We were shocked when she told us that the cheapest apartment available at the time was a one-bedroom unit located at Valley View Apartments in Eagan, MN, costing $400 per month. The apartment had four hundred square feet of living space, and paying that much for a small apartment was unheard of. As it turned out, we had no choice; we had to accept the small apartment and pay that ridiculous price.

We signed a lease and moved into the apartment in June 1989. We lived in that one-bedroom apartment with Jacob sleeping on the living room couch, but he was okay with that. At the time, this was the best we could afford for living accommodations, and it was challenging for us to pay our house mortgage in Amite and rent.

Our apartment was located on the second floor of the building, so we moved in. Linda made it her thing and turned it into our new home. She made that little apartment tolerable for us, and it wasn't so bad. We had our cat Sam with us, and she was also trying to get accustomed to apartment living. We were all experiencing culture shock, and although we lived in Marfa, moving to Minneapolis was an entirely different experience.

Linda, Jacob, and I created our pathway in life and took on the world. After we moved in, on a cold, frigid day in October, we received some snow, which accumulated to about three inches. The snow had piled up on the patio deck, and Sam was looking out of the patio sliding glass door at the snow, wondering what the white stuff was. I opened the sliding glass door to see if she would go out, but she said no way while looking up at me. So, I gently picked her up and dropped her in the snow on the patio, but when she landed with all four paws, she bounced back into the apartment without disturbing those four paw holes. It was so funny, and when she came inside, she went and hid from us for a while. The poor girl had never seen real snow, and as far as she was concerned, if she never saw it again, it would be okay with her.

We were doing quite well in our little apartment, and fortunately, approximately six months later, a co-worker told me she had a friend with a two-bedroom townhouse for rent at 8329 144th Street in Apple Valley, MN., just south of the airport. The rent for this place was about the same as what we were paying for our apartment. We eventually decided to lease the townhouse and lived there until we ultimately relocated to Houston.

U.S. Immigration Inspector Position/Description

Working at the international airport was a valuable learning experience. There, I learned how to enforce U.S. Immigration laws regarding foreign nationals attempting entry into the United States and narcotics smuggling.

I quickly discovered that as an Immigration Inspector, there was a great deal to learn. I wanted to know and understand everything so that I would feel like I was making a meaningful contribution and helping the other inspectors. It didn't take long before I felt ready to dive in to start making cases. I found that studying immigration law, although intriguing, was very complicated. It didn't take me long to figure things out, and I began to learn quickly and easily. The more immigration-related cases I got involved in, the easier everything became for me to understand.

Immigration Inspection Program

A U.S. immigration inspector must inspect all individuals seeking to enter the United States at a U.S. Port of Entry

(POE).

Immigration Inspectors must then determine the nationality and identity of each applicant applying for admission to the U.S. and also prevent the entry of ineligible foreign nationals, including those with criminal, terrorist, or drug trafficking backgrounds, among others. U.S. citizens are automatically admitted upon verification of their citizenship; foreign nationals are questioned, and their documents are examined to determine admissibility based on the requirements of the U.S. immigration law.

The Immigration and Nationality Act (INA) states that an immigration Inspector may question, under oath, any person coming into the United States to determine his or her admissibility. Additionally, an immigration inspector has the authority to search the person and determine the effects of any person seeking admission when there is reason to believe that grounds for exclusion from the U.S. exist that would be disclosed by the search.

The mission of the immigration inspection program is to control and guard the United States' boundaries and borders against the illegal entry of aliens. Immigration Inspectors prevent the entry of terrorists, drug traffickers, criminals, and other persons who may subvert the national interest. They deter illegal immigration by detecting fraudulent documents and entry schemes. Inspectors also initiate prosecutions against individuals who attempt or aid and abet unlawful entry.

At the port of entry, Immigration Inspectors examine individuals and their documents to determine if they are eligible for entry. An example is a visiting foreign national, upon arrival at a U.S. port of entry (POE), who must present their passport and other required documents to enter the United States. You cannot enter the U.S. until you have successfully passed through Immigration Inspection and an inspector has placed an admission stamp in your passport. In some cases, they may be subject to a secondary U.S. immigration inspection to verify their eligibility to enter the United States.

Detailed to Portal, ND

On August 14, 1989, I was detailed to Portal to assist immigration inspectors on the North Dakota-Canadian border. The inspectors told me to be careful when driving up to Portal, as I might miss it if I drove too fast. I laughed it off and began my drive. I went for thirty days and helped until they could fill a few available positions.

I drove from Apple Valley to Portal and got there late that afternoon. While looking for the Portal Port of Entry, I approached the Canadian Immigration inspection booth because I was now entering Canada! I explained to the Canadian Immigration Inspector who I was and what I attempted to do. He laughed at me and told me to turn around while he showed me where the U.S. Immigration POE was located. When I finally found the POE in Portal, I met some inspectors standing there, laughing at me because the Canadian inspector had called them. After the laughing, we planned for me to start work the following day. I went over to the hotel and checked in. I was so tired that I don't remember eating dinner that night.

Working there was quite different from working inspections on the southern border or even working at the POE in Minneapolis. The concept of the inspection process was the same, and today's process has not changed.

On the southern border, people are illegally crossing, attempting to be undetected so they can work, earn money, and stay in the U.S. illegally. Some attempted to smuggle assorted drugs and people across the border.

On the Canadian border, Canadians crossing over from Canada into Portal came daily to shop at the grocery stores or go into Minot, ND, to do shopping. Almost every day, you would encounter the same Canadians crossing the border. Portal and Minot were the two largest cities they could travel to without difficulties because larger cities in Canada, such as

Portal, were a greater distance away.

When I visited, Portal was a small town with approximately 120 residents. It had one small restaurant that sold steaks. If you bought a steak, you took it to the back porch and cooked it yourself in a fire pit. If you did not know how to cook the steak, someone was always there to assist you.

(Left is the Portal Port of Entry on the Canadian border.)

One day in August, Linda and Jacob drove up to Portal to visit me. We decided to take a ride to the northern border.

We drove to Regina, Canada, the capital of the province of Saskatchewan, which has a population of around 226,400.

The Royal Canadian Mounted Police (RCMP) were stationed in Regina, Saskatchewan. We spent the day in Regina as tourists, even bringing our cat, Sam. She was not particularly impressed with Canada and spent most of her time sleeping.

It was nice to see Regina and the place where the Royal Mounted Police train and prepare for duty.

While in Regina, we had our photo taken in Royal Canadian Mounted Police uniforms. The funny sign said, "Saskatchewan Home of the Mounties."

My 30-day detail to Portal ended on September 14, 1989, when I returned home to Apple Valley. That detail taught me that not everything has to be so mechanical; sometimes, you can think outside the box and be more understanding. I learned to go with the flow.

The Capital of Saskatchewan)

In a place like Portal, you can do your job, but be aware that you also live there, and everyone in the vicinity is likely a relative, friend, neighbor, or coworker. The people you encounter and the reason for the encounter would guide you in managing that situation.

Working in Portal taught me that the people there were regular human beings just living their lives among themselves, not bothering anyone. They all knew one another, and most people were related. Catching young people trying to sneak in across the border in the trunks of vehicles meant you called their parents and sent them back. You did not have to arrest them and put them in jail, which would have resulted in a criminal record that they would never be able to erase.

People came over and pulled into our port of entry daily to have coffee with us or even bring us donuts or bagels. I quickly learned that you were dealing with a family environment in Portal, where you enforce the law while being reasonable at the same time.

After returning to work in Minneapolis, I often thought about Portal and the way of life there. The slow pace and the lack of significant problems or issues regarding immigration made it tempting to consider working there permanently.

The Canadian Immigration inspectors would walk over and have coffee, and we would do the same. I liked that thought, but I realized that most people working in immigration were from the area or nearby, so they adapted to the surroundings more easily. I didn't know how I would fit into that environment. You had to be from that area to adjust and fit in. I had to return to reality in Minneapolis, where I dealt with foreign nationals arriving from many countries, trying to make their way into the U.S. for various reasons. Although most people were legitimate, there were those seeking entry who had ulterior motives, and you must remain vigilant for them.

Firearms Instructor

On August 6, 1990, I attended the Firearms Instructor Training Program in Artesia, NM, and graduated from the course on August 17, 1990. As a collateral duty, I was assigned as the firearms instructor for the Minneapolis inspections program. I scheduled and maintained quarterly firearms qualifications, and if someone needed help or training to qualify, I would work with them to help them become proficient in using their service weapons.

Processing Russian Nationals

Another duty I performed in Minneapolis was processing applications from Russian nationals seeking benefits or refugee status. Once a month, several immigration inspectors visit the processing center at one of the international charities hosting the events. The charity programs represented the Russians in the Northern Minnesota area who were seeking employment and a new life.

There were numerous other reasons for the Russian processing, but they were all related to obtaining refugee status. They were waiting for a family member to petition for them, or they were fleeing violence, persecution, and war in Russia.

Immigration Examiner Position

In May of 1991, I was offered the opportunity to transfer from the Inspections program to the Examination Program as an Immigration Examiner assigned to the Adjudication Branch of U.S. Immigration. I was assigned to investigate marriage and visa fraud cases by conducting extensive interviews with individuals who had been called into the office.

I also adjudicated applications and petitions for various U.S. visas, including marriage and naturalization applications for U.S. Citizenship. I investigated marriage fraud cases in which U.S. Citizens married foreign nationals to help them obtain permanent resident status.

On the left is our first apartment in Eagan, MN, and on the

right is our second apartment, a townhouse in Apple Valley, MN.

Here is a picture of Jacob and me patiently waiting for the gates to open. Go Twins! I enjoyed going downtown to the Minnesota Twins games with Jacob. We always arrived early to be among the first inside the park when the gates opened. We would always watch the pre-game and batting practice.

I always enjoyed watching pitchers warm up before a game and was amazed at the time they took and the preparation they put in to loosen up and get ready to pitch. As I watched the pitchers loosen up and throw, I took good notes because Jacob was a pitcher, and I would later show Jacob the techniques that the pros were using.

I also recall that Jacob and I once attended a Minnesota North Stars hockey game. It was quite enjoyable to watch, and I vividly recall that night. We had intended to attend a Minnesota Timberwolves basketball game, but never did.

Travis Tritt

One day, while I was at work, Linda and Jacob attended the grand opening of a Target store in Apple Valley, Minnesota.

Linda went to meet Tritt, and Jacob was her photographer. Tritt was present for the grand opening and conducted a meet-and-greet.

Linda wanted Tritt's autograph, so she brought along one of her CD covers for Tritt to sign. Linda said that when they said hello to one another, Tritt said, "Hey, you're not from here," and Linda responded, "No, I'm a Louisiana girl."

A Choking Baby

One day, while I was off work, Linda, Jacob, and I went to the Target store to shop. Walking into the store, I saw a woman screaming, and numerous people gathered around her, looking at something. As I walked over to see what was happening, I noticed the woman holding a tiny baby turning blue. I recognized that the baby was choking on something, so I reached in to grab the baby and help. I knew we needed to clear the baby's airway. Well, the woman resisted and would not give me the baby. She was holding on tight and would not let go. I was able to get the baby away from her, and I immediately tried to dislodge what was lodged in its throat. I patted the baby's back several times with a little force and then shook it; that was when a small gumball object popped out of its mouth.

As soon as the baby started breathing again, the woman grabbed the baby back from me and ran out of the store to the parking lot. Hopefully, she took the baby to a hospital, but I never found that out.

The store manager walked up and thanked me, but the woman never said anything to me. I was glad that I went to the store that day because, with everyone just standing around staring at the baby doing nothing, the baby could have died. Hopefully, the baby grew up and had a long, happy life.

Carson Pierre Scott

While in Apple Valley, Linda decided to look for employment one day. She visited a Carson Pierre Scott department store at Burnsville Mall in Burnsville, MN. The store was close to our home and would not be a bad drive for her. She applied for employment and was hired on the same day.

Linda was so pretty; how could you not hire her? She went to work there and made many new friends. One good friend she made was Barb Street.

In the photo, Linda and Barb is wearing a Halloween costume while working. Linda is dressed as a credit card named "Born A. Shopper." HA! She made that costume! Barb later left the store and moved to Duluth, MN, and Linda made numerous trips there to visit her.

Linda also became friends with another co-worker, Rosalie Knecht. They became good friends and decided to introduce me to her husband, Jim. We all became friends and met up on occasion.

For our sixteenth wedding anniversary, Rosalie and Jim took us on the Minnesota Zephyr dinner train;

unfortunately, the train is no longer in service today. The train was located in Stillwater, MN. It was a big tourist attraction at the time. It operated as a dinner train, serving a five-course, white linen dinner on a six-mile route, traveling at speeds of four to seven miles per hour. It had two locomotives, with one on each end of the train.

The train consisted of five restored dining cars that traveled along the St. Croix River bluffs, then turned westward and followed a stream. The train traveled six miles before stopping, then six miles back. The entire trip lasted approximately three and a half hours. It was an outstanding train ride and a sumptuous anniversary dinner for us. The photo above shows the dining table.

Linda's mom, Dorothy (D-Dot) Alford lived in Amite, while we were in Apple Valley. One day, she came to visit us during the winter of 1989. While she was with us, we had a decent amount of snowfall, and it was freezing cold during her stay. D-Dot was a good sport; she played with Jacob in the snow several times. She took walks with us around the neighborhood in the snow, never complaining. I could never convince her to wear skates for ice skating. However, I never blamed her because I had never done it myself.

Youth Baseball

While in Minnesota, Jacob and I participated in the recreation youth baseball program. Jacob played on several different teams and even attended a baseball camp hosted by the recreational league in Apple Valley. I was the head coach for one of the teams Jacob played on, and we had a successful year. The only issue I found with playing baseball in Apple Valley was that you had a small window of time to play for the season. The weather changed quickly, and other sports were about to start. You had approximately six weeks to play baseball, with ten games scheduled.

Another issue you had to consider was the other sports being sponsored by the city. As soon as the baseball program was wrapping up, basketball, football, and hockey were starting up. Many of the young men on your team loved baseball, but they also loved the option of playing hockey and other sports. Jacob was the only player on the team committed to the one sport of baseball, and he was not interested in playing hockey or football. The baseball season was reasonably short for those reasons.

I remember that during the summertime, the red clay dirt on the baseball field was so hard that it was as if the ground had never thawed out. For baseball, it made sliding around the bases complex for the kids, even tearing their pants and hurting their knees. Kids were always getting hurt playing in the northern dirt. My time in Minnesota ended in July 1991, and I transferred to Houston, Texas, as an Immigration Inspector.

(Jacob is taking pitching Instructions at a clinic in Apple Valley while I stand watching in the red shirt.)

The opportunity to transfer became I wanted to return to the South, closer to our hometown area. Houston would be a stepping stone to achieving that goal. Besides, Jacob and Linda were ready for a much warmer climate anyway. Well, me too!

Here's the thing: if you're going to live near Minneapolis, you'd better learn to love winter; otherwise, you'll be in for a rude awakening. I remember the winter being long because of the cold and depressing gray skies. Winters in Minneapolis were rough. Living there, you must learn to embrace winter fully.

We never got involved in winter sports, but learned about proper clothing layering. If you don't learn to love winter, you'll be miserable and cooped up inside for months, which isn't fun for anyone.

Let's go to Houston, where it's warmer.

CHAPTER 10

Houston, Texas

On June 16, 1991, I transferred from Minneapolis to Houston, Texas, as an Immigration Inspector, the same position I held in Minneapolis when I first arrived there. The opportunity presented itself for me to transfer back into the inspections branch for U.S. Immigration, and this move was an

opportunity to get us closer to the South, closer to home.

After receiving my official transfer papers, we packed our belongings in Apple Valley and headed to Houston. Upon arriving in Houston, we stayed in a hotel and searched for a place to rent. We eventually found a house for rent located at 49 S. Brookberry Ct., Woodlands, Texas (Left). The Woodlands was a brand-new development project located in the north of Houston, with only a few homes already built in the area known as Panther Creek. The Woodlands' goal was to develop the area into a self-contained city with grocery stores and gas stations. The plan was for residents of The Woodlands not to have to leave the area for anything. It would be a City within itself.

This house had plenty of room for us and a huge backyard, and it was located in a great neighborhood. We didn't care much about the garage entrance in front of the house, but we didn't know how long we would live there. I would see how the position worked out and if we liked living in that area. However, for now, the house would be okay.

We made several friends in the neighborhood. Two young women lived across the street from us, and their names were Cindy and Cindy—yes, both Cindy. They had a black-and-white cat with fur that resembled a tuxedo, so they named him Tuxedo. We became good friends with them and did many things together.

Immigration Inspection Program

As I previously explained in other chapters, individuals seeking entry into the United States are inspected at Ports of Entry (POEs) by immigration inspectors who determine their admissibility. The inspection process encompasses work concerning the entry of aliens and U.S. citizens into the United States.

I worked as an immigration inspector at the Houston International Airport and, on occasion, at one of the two seaports. I performed the same duties in Houston as I did in Minneapolis inspections. I conducted inspections of foreign nationals attempting to enter the U.S. from numerous countries. The difference is that Houston received flights worldwide because it was much larger than Minneapolis. In Minneapolis, we processed three to five international flights daily; in Houston, we processed over a hundred.

Two major seaports received foreign vessels daily, arriving at all hours of the day and night. It was common to be assigned to inspect a foreign vessel scheduled to arrive at any hour of the day or night, but most of the ships scheduled never arrived on time at the port.

Ships would come and wait in the harbor for a place to dock. Sometimes, a ship could take several days to be docked and inspected. There were a few occasions when we would meet the ship in the harbor and go onboard to inspect the crew, and U.S. Customs would board with us to inspect the vessel's contents.

Football

Jacob played football for the first time while living in Houston, and he played for his middle school team, which he attended in The Woodlands. Baseball season was over, so when he asked me, I said, ' Sure, give it a shot. I would occasionally watch him practice, and I was able to make the most of his games.

There was one game where Jacob entered the game as a running back. I was standing on the sidelines when Jacob broke out of the huddle, looked at me, and started pointing to himself. When he did that, I believe everyone else from the other team saw him pointing as well, because when the ball was snapped and handed off, the other team was on him like white on rice. I was doing everything I

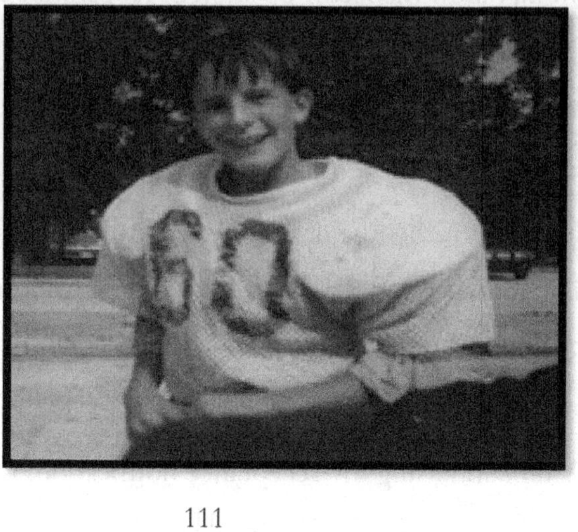

could to laugh, but I also felt sorry for him. Anyway, I don't believe he ever did that again.

I was so proud that Jacob tried football, as he had never played. Maybe if he had stuck with it, who knows? I encouraged him to focus more on baseball than football, but I believed he was okay with it.

The above photo is of Jacob's football team. He is standing in the middle, looking back at his mom, who is taking his picture. I was proud of Jacob for everything he attempted to do.

Senior Inspector in Miami

After several months in Houston, I was notified that I had been selected for a senior immigration inspector position in Miami. While in Minneapolis, I submitted my applications for the open Senior Inspector position in Miami and the Immigration Inspector position in Houston. I was selected for the Houston position, and I never heard anything about the Miami position, so I forgot about it.

On November 3, 1991, I received notice that I had been selected for the Miami position and was requested to respond. The Senior Immigration Inspector position would be a promotion and a salary upgrade for me. I responded to the Port Director in Miami, stating that I had accepted the position.

After submitting my acceptance notification, I had to wait for the official travel orders to cover my move expenses and set a date to report for duty. Once I received my official move orders, Linda, Jacob, and I packed up again and prepared to move to Miami.

Moving away was a significant life event filled with mixed emotions. It was a time of excitement, anticipation, and, often, a bit of sadness for us. With our friends and my co-workers, we laughed together and even complained together about anything and everything. Many times, we stressed together and celebrated many things together. I made friends with numerous coworkers and was sad to see this chapter of my life end. However, I was also excited to see what the future held. They say all good things must end, but saying goodbye to such good friends and coworkers was sad.

Going Away Party

After I informed everyone in Houston that I was accepting a position in Miami, all of my co-workers got together and threw Linda and me a going-away party. Although I was only briefly in Houston, I made many good friends at the airport and felt well-liked. I got along remarkably with everyone at work and enjoyed the work. I would have been very happy working in Houston if I had not been selected for the Senior Inspector position.

One of my going-away presents was a praying cowboy, shown in the picture above, which I still display in my study today. Along with the cowboy, I was given a "Texas Passport," which I still have.

Although our stay in Houston was brief, we had a great time, learned many new things, and met some wonderful people. Jacob even got to experience a couple of new things while there, like playing football.

In January 1992, I started my new position in Miami as a Senior Immigration Inspector.

Off to sunny Miami, Florida!

Chapter 11

Miami, Florida

On November 3, 1991, I transferred to Miami as a Senior Immigration Inspector assigned to conduct criminal prosecutions at Miami International Airport. When we first arrived in Miami, we stayed at the Quality Inn Hotel on Old U.S. HWY 1 until we decided where to purchase or build a new house.

Before arriving in Miami, I had

spoken extensively with Senior Immigration Inspector Dan Tarasevich, who worked there. Dan knew I was leaving Houston and coming to Miami because Dan was the acting supervisor for the Miami office.

He and I became good friends, and when I arrived in Miami, he would pick me up every morning for work and bring me home in the afternoons. Dan did not live far from our hotel, so he was happy to give me a ride. We stayed at the hotel until we could find a house or have one built.

In November 1991, we found an area where we wanted to live, and construction was started on our new home, which was built in Cutler Ridge, FL, in a subdivision called Lakes by the Bay. Cutler Ridge was located near the airport office, providing easy access to and from work. (22260 SW 121st Street, Miami, and we moved in March 1992)

Dan lived in a subdivision next to ours, and we often visited each other.

Our new home in Lakes by the Bay was pictured before Hurricane Andrew visited us. Although we were only there for a brief period, we made many friends in the neighborhood, and Jacob made several of his friends who lived down the street from us.

This was Linda's pink house, with plenty of room for us to

spread out and enjoy. Our only issue was the garage entry in front of the house. We didn't care for the large front entry garage door.

Saving a Duckling

In Lakes by the Bay, a large walking track surrounds one of the lakes on the property, which is not far from our house. Some afternoons, we would take walks around the lake.

One day, Linda and I decided to take a walk. As we walked around the track, the weather began to turn nasty, with the wind picking up and blowing, while the clouds darkened and grew ominous. It appeared to be getting ready to storm, and we would try to get back to the house before it arrived.

As we walked, I noticed a mama duck looking out at the lake, and several little ducklings were standing around her. I looked out at the lake, and several hundred yards offshore, I could see a little duckling bobbing up and down in the water. It did not appear as if the duckling would make it, and I was worried that the waves would overtake it and cause it to drown. The mama was quacking loudly, but the little duckling could not reach the shore.

I removed my shoes, waded into the water, and swam to where the duckling was bobbing. It took me a few minutes to get to it, but when I did, I could tell it had no strength left to swim.

It was just barely able to float on top of the water. When I reached to grab it, I recalled that it didn't resist. I believe it was glad to see me. I held on to it and swam back to shore. The waves grew rough, and swimming back became difficult, but we managed to make it.

I took the duckling and stood it by its mom. The mom gathered all her other ducklings and began quacking as she walked away from the water. It made me feel so good to do that, and I know that if I had not gone out there to retrieve the duckling, it would have drowned.

Hurricane Andrew

After only five months of living in our new home, Hurricane Andrew paid us a visit on August 24, 1992, and destroyed our new home and belongings. The entire area in South Florida was devastated by the storm.

When we heard that the storm was heading our way, we had friends who lived nearby. She worked for the Army Intelligence Division in Homestead, FL, located at the Air Reserve Base. With the storm coming, she invited us to stay with them on the base to ride out the storm. We all figured it would be a better place to stay during the storm instead of our homes.

Homestead is located approximately twenty-six miles south of

Miami, and we decided to stay with them because, at the time, Andrew was anticipated to make landfall north of Miami. Going to Homestead would put us further away from the storm in a safer area. On the night of the storm, we went to Homestead and settled into the three-story building on the base. We started watching the weather on TV following the

storm track, and as time passed, Andrew made a southward turn and was now tracking toward making landfall near Homestead. Since we were settled and secured inside the building, we decided to stay there and ride out the storm.

Andrew came and made its way on shore at Elliott Key near

Homestead as a Category 5 at landfall, and it was one hell of a storm.

During the storm, we watched out the windows and saw my red Nissan pick-up blown by the wind across an area of the parking lot. I had a black toolbox bolted to the back of my truck, but after the storm, when I was finally able to access my truck, the toolbox was missing. We also watched several other vehicles blown around the parking lot because it was later determined that the storm winds exceeded two hundred mph. When Hurricane Andrew's eye passed us, the winds diminished, and we could see the stars in the night sky. This lasted approximately twenty minutes before the wind began to return and conditions worsened.

By mid-morning the next day, we could go outside as the winds and rain had subsided. Several of us returned to Cutler Ridge to inspect our homes and assess the damage. As we left Homestead, we drove north on the interstate, and I recall the high water on the road being so profound that, at times, we had to take turns walking out in front of the vehicle to ensure we stayed on the roadway.

We drove for several hours before arriving at our subdivision because everything was unrecognizable. The trees were down everywhere, and all the houses were destroyed. The streets were almost impassable in vehicles, so we had to drive across yards and take our chances. When we eventually found our neighborhood, or what was left of it, our homes were heavily damaged, with some destroyed. Our house was approximately 70% damaged, but we had one bedroom with a solid roof still intact.

We stayed in that one bedroom because the National Guard closed the area at night to prevent looting. During the daytime, we met our neighbors outside and took turns cooking on the grill while we all waited for our insurance adjusters to come by for appraisals. Additionally, the Red Cross was in the area, providing meals of beans and hot dogs to all those staying at home.

We waited for a State Farm adjuster to come, and we had to put our information on the garage door. It was later reported that Hurricane Andrew was the strongest and most devastating hurricane on record to hit southern Florida. Andrew caused billions of dollars in damage, with Homestead being the most severely affected community. As Category 5 at landfall, it had a maximum sustained wind of 165 mph.

North to Broward County

Our insurance was with State Farm, which eventually settled our claim. We packed up what we had left and moved north to Broward County because the recovery south of Miami was expected to take an exceptionally long time.

In Broward County, we could lease an apartment at Winner's

Circle Apartments in Parkland, FL, until we decided where we wanted to rebuild. We eventually found a suitable location to build, and in September, construction began on our new home in Margate, FL. We lived in the apartment while we built our new home. Pictured below is Winner Circle Apartments.

I fished in the lake surrounding the apartment complex and caught plenty of bass, but always threw them back. I caught many Peacock Bass, colorful fish with a large black spot on their tails. Fishing served as a release from work pressures, rebuilding a new home, and dealing with life's personal challenges. Walking outside, sitting on the lake's bank, and relaxing was nice. We enjoyed living there while our house was built and made friends there.

Cypress Cove Subdivision

In March 1993, after a six-month building process, our new home in Cypress Cove Subdivision at 7381 Viscaya Circle, Margate, was completed, and we moved in. It was a great community with friendly people, and we made many friends. Cypress Cove was a gated community of single-family homes located at the southwest corner of Royal Palm Blvd and Rock Island Rd. in Margate.

(Pictured above is our Margate home)

After moving into our new home, we registered Jacob in high school, and he started his freshman year at Stoneman Douglas High School in Parkland, FL.

After his sophomore year, Jacob transferred to Florida Bible Christian Academy (FBCA) in Broward County for his junior year. Jacob enjoyed the baseball program at Florida Bible, led by his coach, Eddie Martinez, who was once affiliated with the Cleveland Indians. Jacob finished his junior year before we transferred to Atlanta.

Jacob

Senior Immigration Inspector

When I began working as a Senior Inspector at Miami International Airport, it didn't take me long to learn my actual duties. I was assigned to investigate and present criminal prosecution cases generated from the airport and seaport inspections program. These cases involved illegal re-entry after deportation, visa fraud, marriage benefit fraud, and false claims of U.S. citizenship.

On average, I presented to the U.S. Attorney in Miami for twenty or more monthly prosecutions. The conviction rate was

100% because most pleaded guilty to being deported from the U.S. and returning home.

Tropic Star

The Tropic Star cruise line operated out of Miami and sailed twice a week to the Bahamas. On Tuesdays, it sailed to Bimini, and on Thursdays, to Freeport.

The U.S. Immigration Service was responsible for inspecting all passengers and crew arriving on the ship returning from the Bahamas. To assist the cruise lines, an immigration inspector sailed with the boat from Miami to the Bahamas and inspected all the passengers before returning to Miami. This process streamlined the disembarking of passengers upon arrival back in Miami, especially when it was late at night.

I conducted the inspections for the Tropic Star whenever I was assigned, and most of the time, I worked on both Tuesday and Thursday cruises. Working the cruise was enjoyable because it got me out of the office for the day; it was a lovely sail on open blue water, and conducting the inspections was not difficult. Plus, the food served on the cruise was incredibly good, too.

Upon leaving the port, the ship's chief steward brought me all the passports for the passengers and crew members. Upon receiving them, I would review each passport to ensure all were in order so there would be no issues upon our return when we left the Bahamas.

I would happily volunteer to work at the Tropic Star whenever possible, especially when family or friends visit us from out of town. The cruise line encouraged me to bring a guest, and I often brought Linda or both Linda and Jacob.

Linda and Jacob are on board

As I said, the Tropic Star encouraged me to bring a guest, so on numerous occasions, in addition to Linda and Jacob, I brought Linda's mom, D-Dot, and many of our friends from Louisiana on trips.

Linda, Jacob, and one of Jacob's friends took this trip to Freeport. On the way over, Linda and I were walking around the ship, just relaxing, when I got a page from the Chief Steward asking me to come to the casino immediately. I remember walking to the casino, thinking there must be an issue with one of the passengers, but when I arrived, Jacob and his friend were standing with the Chief Steward. Chief Steward explained that Jacob and his friend were playing on the slot machines and had won some money. She explained that she could not pay them because they were underage, and they should not have been playing. While laughing, she asked me not to allow them back into the casino. I explained to the boys that they were too young to play and had to stay out of the casino area.

Later, we all laughed about the incident at the casino, and I didn't get upset about it. My only question is how much they won. I never found out, and neither did Jacob nor his friend.

Me and Linda

On the return to Miami, an excellent dinner was served, and several shows were performed in the ship's theaters and lounges, including singing, dancing, magicians, and acrobats. One of the lounges also showed movies.

Inspecting the Tropic Star was fun and relaxing in many ways, and the crew did everything possible to make the voyage a good one.

Linda and I are in the picture on the left, and the photo on the right shows me conducting inspections. My pretty assistant, my "bodyguard," sat beside me on this trip.

Several years after leaving Miami, I heard that the Tropic Star had ceased its cruises and relocated to operate elsewhere outside the South Pacific. I tried checking on the ship's status and found nothing. Someone told me it had sunk near the Philippines, but I could never confirm that story.

Jacob and Baseball

Jacob played baseball with several recreational league teams in Margate while also playing for the junior high school team at Stoneman Douglas High until he transferred to Florida Bible Christian Academy, a private school in Broward County, after his sophomore year.

Jacob played and pitched his junior year at Florida Bible, and the team had a great season. Jacob liked his head coach, Ed Martinez, who was affiliated with the Cleveland Indians.

During the off-season, Jacob attended the Playball Baseball Academy in Fort Lauderdale, which was owned and operated by Randy Kierce. Randy's father-in-law was Fred Ferreira, who oversaw international operations for the Major League Baseball team, the Montreal Expos. Randy was also an international scout, and he worked out players at the academy who were hoping to secure a professional baseball contract.

Jacob practiced and played in games with numerous professional players who were attending their rehabilitation at the academy. He was once invited to play on a team sponsored by the Playball Baseball Academy to travel to Curacao for a tournament. Many other major league teams also represented and participated in the tournament. The tournament provided another opportunity for professional teams to rehab their players and offer them some off-season playing time to get back in shape. Some teams use it to showcase players for trades or signings.

Jacob was a pitcher and was invited to travel with the team for the experience. Hopefully, he will pitch an inning or two in a game with professional players. Most players in the tournament were professional players rehabilitating from an injury and getting back into playing shape.

While Jacob and the Playball Academy team were in Curacao, they were preparing to play in a game when a coach from one of the teams approached Jacob's coach, Randy Kierce, and asked to borrow a pitcher that he could use for an inning. The coach explained that some of their pitchers were flying in that day and were running late. Understand that this tournament allowed players to showcase their talent and return to playing shape from injuries.

Randy loaned Jacob to join the other team and assist them with their pitching. The Atlanta Braves represented the team and used Jacob to start the game. He was assigned to pitch for an inning or two before being relieved, but fortunately, he was doing so well that they allowed him to continue pitching, completing five innings.

After the game, Jacob was asked to give a television interview about his experience pitching in the tournament, and the interview went well. We have a copy of that interview on a VHS tape, which we are immensely proud of.

Go Marlins!

If you are going to live in Miami, you must be a Florida Marlins fan. The Marlins began playing as an expansion team in 1993.

They originally played their home games at Joe Robbie Stadium, so we attended games whenever possible and always had a great time. Of course, we always had to arrive early to watch batting practice and warm-ups. In the picture, Jacob and I attended Marlin's game during their inaugural year, and we were lucky to have such a pretty lady with her shades sitting with us.

Immigration Training

While stationed in Miami, I attended numerous training

seminars and classes by federal and local law enforcement agencies.

On August 21, 1992, I attended the Airport Investigator School at the Metropolitan Police Institute in Miami-Dade County, Florida. We were taught interview and interrogation techniques and how to properly gather and preserve evidence for criminal prosecution cases. We were introduced to and fired assorted handguns, rifles, and shotguns. We participated in extensive physical techniques and hand-to-hand defense.

On October 31, 1994, I attended a two-week Senior Immigration Inspector class in Artesia, NM. I graduated on November 17, 1994.

The class concentrated on the senior inspector's program for conducting and preparing criminal prosecution cases. The courses instructed on collecting evidence, completing proper paperwork, and preparing a criminal case for presentation to an assistant U.S. attorney for criminal prosecution.

Since the training lasted two weeks, we had to stay over the weekend, so we took the opportunity to tour the surrounding area of Artesia. We visited Roswell, Carlsbad, and the caverns, then drove to the Lincoln National Forest, which was a delightful place to see, but I wouldn't want to live there.

My co-worker, Alicia Benevidez, was a Senior Inspector in

Miami and attended the school. Over the years we worked together, she and I became remarkably close friends. Several years after I left Miami, I learned that Alicia had developed breast cancer and eventually passed away. Alicia was fun; she and I worked on many criminal cases together. I have always enjoyed working with her.

I also met many senior inspectors from around the country at the school, including two guys I became good friends with from the Honolulu, Hawaii, office. They were Ben Bumanglag and Randy Hammer, and they were completely nuts. Randy looked just like Hulk Hogan, the wrestler, and you always had to keep your eyes on him because he loved pulling tricks and pranks on people.

Meeting all these Senior Inspectors gave me a terrific opportunity to network with one another and share information and ideas. We discussed the prosecution process and how our offices manage criminal cases. By doing this, we Sometimes, pick up innovative ideas to bring back to your offices and incorporate into your prosecution program.

In the afternoons, we had self-defense classes, and we paired off in groups of three. Randy, Ben, and I formed a group, and we had to take turns wearing the Iron Man suit, which was protective gear one of us wore while the other two practiced self-defense techniques on him. The one wearing the protective suit got the hell beaten out of him, and we beat on each other so hard that we could not help but laugh, causing the instructor to intervene and break us up.

In the photo, Alicia is in the front row, far right, and I am in the second row, second from left. Ben is in the second row, first from left, and Randy is in the center back row.

As I previously mentioned, Ben and Randy were two crazy guys, but look at Ben's last name and tell me we did not have fun with that. We nicknamed Randy "Hammer Time."

Randy was tall, so hitting him was like punching a tree, but we had so much fun that others in our class wanted to join our group. We wouldn't let them.

Randy always carried a small camera, taking pictures of anything and everything. Once, I went to the restroom, and while there, someone said, "Hey," so I turned around quickly, and Randy took a picture of me. I have a copy of that picture in my photo album.

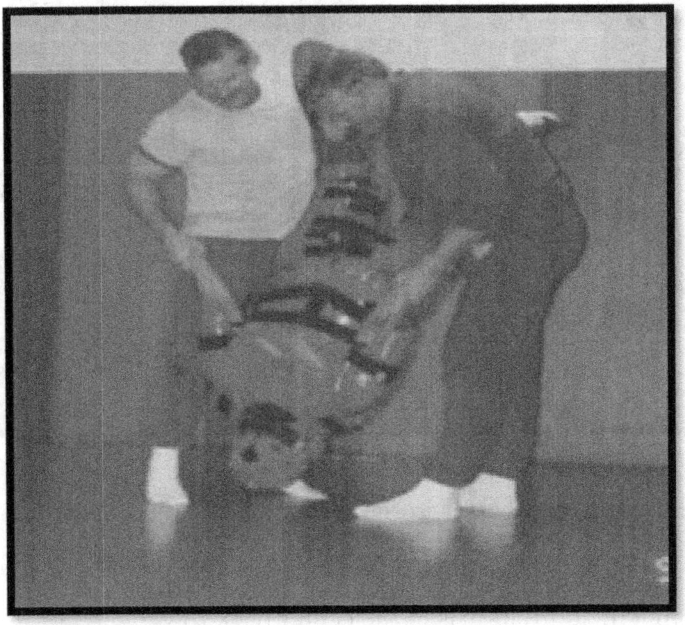

We all stayed in contact over the years, but eventually, I lost contact with them. In the photo, Randy and I are banging Ben's head on the floor. The instructor got after us and almost threw us out of the class because he thought we were trying to hurt Ben. Ben did tell us he couldn't see straight for a while, but he recovered.

Firearms Instructor School

On August 6, 1990, I attended the Firearms Instructor Training Course in Artesia, NM, to become the head firearms instructor for the Miami U.S. Immigration Inspections branch. I made some good friends in the firearms class, and Dan Tarasevich attended the same school.

Upon returning to Miami, I began conducting all the firearms training and qualifications for inspections at the outdoor range at the Krome Detention Facility. About a year later, I obtained an indoor range for our qualifications at the Coast Guard facility located at the seaport. I would schedule an entire week to conduct our qualifications and ensure that I have all the inspectors qualified and that my certifications are sent to the district office. Inspectors worked numerous shifts day and night, and some were always on details. I had to reschedule them when they had opportunities to qualify.

The Coast Guard had a new, up-to-date indoor shooting range at its seaport office. On days when I scheduled range dates, they provided me with complete access to the facility, and I was also able to schedule or reschedule whenever I needed. Many days, the Coast Guard staff worked around the seaport office. They would have lunch brought into the facility.

They consistently requested that I join them for lunch, and I was happy to comply. When I had time between qualifications and no one was scheduled to qualify, the Coast Guard would provide me with fishing rods and reels, and I would sit out on the dock and fish. I enjoyed serving as the firearms instructor in Miami and appreciated the Coast Guard personnel, who treated me well.

Before I left Miami, Dan volunteered to assist me in the firearms program, which he took over when I transferred to Atlanta.

Leaving Miami

An opportunity arose for me to transfer to Atlanta Immigration Inspections, where I would work as a Special Operations Inspector assigned to Hartsfield International Airport. I decided to apply for the position and was lucky enough to be selected.

I enjoyed my work in Miami as a Senior Inspector, managing the prosecution program and conducting daily interviews with foreign nationals. Miami was an excellent training ground for me, where I conducted interviews and interrogations, and I learned a great deal during my time there. I became well-established in Miami and developed a great rapport with the U.S. Attorney's Office.

Leaving Miami was hard for me because we had all made many

friends while living there, and we had so much fun going out to dinner and enjoying the nightlife. We visited all the beaches and soaked up the sun. Still, I had the opportunity to transfer to Atlanta and take on a new position as a Special Operations Inspector, which would further enhance my career. When we drove away from Miami, Jacob's friend, Danny Moore, rode with us from Miami up to Atlanta. They were both great friends and hated departing from one another. They played baseball and did everything together. I will discuss this further later.

Goodbye Miami, hello Atlanta!

Chapter 12

Atlanta, Georgia

In June 1995, while in Miami, I spoke with Willie Anderson, the U.S. Immigration Port Director in Atlanta. I met him at an immigration conference, and we became good friends. Willie told me that he had been hearing a lot about me and my work ethic and would like to have me come work in Atlanta. Willie explained that he had a Special Operations Inspector (SOI) position available and would like me to fill it.

Since I was always looking for new adventures, the position sounded interesting, and I thought Atlanta would be an interesting place to work. After talking it over with Linda, I decided to submit my paperwork for a transfer to Atlanta. Sometime later, Willie called to offer me the position officially, and I accepted.

Finding Our New Home

After I was notified of my selection for Atlanta, Linda and I began our search for a new home online. We eventually found a home in Rayner Woods Subdivision in Newnan, GA., about 35 miles south of Atlanta and the airport. We contacted a realtor from Newnan, who advised us to inspect the house and see it firsthand to determine whether to proceed with the purchase.

After receiving official notification of my selection and travel orders, we took a government-paid trip to Newnan to view the home we were interested in and meet our realtor. When we met our realtor in Newnan, she directed us to the house in the Rayner Woods subdivision. Sadly, upon our arrival at the house, we discovered that it had recently been under contract and was no longer available. That was very disappointing, and we had to start looking all over again.

Since we liked the area in the Rayner Woods subdivision,

our realtor recommended that we explore other homes available in the same neighborhood. We discovered the house in the photo, located at 87 Rayner Drive, just up the street from the initial house we were considering. This house was still under construction but was available for purchase and was expected to be completed soon. After negotiation with the builder, we could put the home under contract. At this stage, Linda was also allowed to select assorted items for the interior decor and add a personal touch.

After finding and securing our new home, we drove back home to Margate to complete our household packing and prepare for our move to Newnan.

The U.S. government had a funded program that covered employees' relocation expenses, including house-hunting searches and all incidental costs associated with moving. The government also offered a home buyout program for homeowners. The program required you to list your home with a realtor to sell, and while on the market, you were allowed to receive three home appraisals from qualified realtors. The government would then offer to purchase your home for the average of the three appraisals. This step was designed to facilitate faster and easier movement, enabling employees to reach their assigned location more quickly and efficiently. We accepted the government's offer to purchase our home, and after our house was packed and loaded into the moving van, we began preparing for our drive to Newnan.

Driving to Newnan

On August 18, 1995, we left our home in Margate and drove to Newnan with Jacob's friend, Danny Moore, who rode with us to keep Jacob company. Danny rode along with Jacob to offer him friendly moral support, as Jacob wasn't happy about leaving Margate. Jacob had made many friends and been involved in numerous activities while living in Margate, and he had reservations about going. Danny was probably his best friend, and it was good that he rode with us.

Upon arriving in Newnan, we had reservations at the Holiday Inn right off Interstate 85, Exit 9. We wanted a place to stay close to the interstate so I could commute to work, and also close enough for us to check on the status of our house construction. We lived at the hotel until we were ready to move into our new home. The hotel was fine, but it was not a home.

On Sunday, August 19th, we decided to take a day to relax and explore the downtown area of Atlanta. We toured the Atlanta Coca-Cola company, among other places, and explored as much of downtown Atlanta as possible that day. While taking in the sights, we learned where everything was located and where we would live in Newnan. That Sunday was fun for us, as it allowed us to relax and release some of the stress we had built up from starting a new job and moving into a new house.

Closing on Our New Home

Finally, on August 31st, we closed on our new home in Rayner Woods, and it was now all ours. After our closing, we had to be patient and wait for the delivery of our furniture. Still, I stayed constantly on the phone with the moving company, negotiating a delivery date for our furniture.

On September 6th, our furniture was delivered to our new home, and the furniture, along with the packed boxes, was placed where Linda had instructed. Then came the chore of unpacking all those boxes, but through time and patience, everything in the boxes was unloaded, and our new house became our home. Of course, Linda added her decorative touches to every room, making the house appear as if it had come straight out of a magazine.

Our home in Rayner Woods was quite spacious, featuring three bedrooms upstairs and a sizable bonus room. We had plenty of space, and Jacob wanted the large bonus room for his bedroom. He used that room until he went to college, and then it became my playroom. I turned it into my man cave, where I hung out, watched TV, and relaxed.

Our home was approximately thirty miles south of the airport, but it was also conveniently close to the international terminal, where I parked my vehicle for work every day. I worked shifts, and my schedule changed every two weeks, so there were specific shifts when I had no traffic to deal with on my commute to and from work. However, one particular shift, early in the morning, was particularly challenging as I tried to get into and out of the airport parking terminal.

When we first moved into our home in Newnan, it had a small-town country atmosphere with hardly any traffic, making it easy to navigate around town. When it turned dark outside, you could walk outside into the backyard, look up, and see bright stars shining. However, after five years of living there, Newnan experienced rapid growth in population and business. Before we left Newnan, looking up at night to see the stars became extremely difficult due to the numerous lights surrounding the city. The city lights in Newnan block the view of the stars. Over the years, Newnan had changed so much that it was no longer the same Newnan we had moved to in 1995.

Baseball

After settling into our new home, we wasted no time getting Jacob involved in the local community baseball programs by trying out for the Peachtree City baseball league. When the league was preparing to get started, they needed coaches, so I was asked to coach one of the teams, and Jacob played on my team. Jacob had much experience pitching for numerous teams in Miami and against professional players, and he dominated the pitching in this league.

With Jacob's help, our team went undefeated in our first season. I had coaches from other teams ask me not to pitch Jacob against them so that they could have a fair chance at winning. I had a rotation for the pitchers on my team, and if your team came up when Jacob was scheduled to pitch against you, then so be it. Tough! Ha! Spoken like an authentic father/coach. I was so proud of Jacob and showed him off every chance I got.

Jacob and Schools

On August 28, 1995, Jacob began his senior year at East Coweta High School in Newnan, where he became a starting pitcher on the high school baseball team under Coach Brett Bramlet. Jacob is in the center row, fourth from left.

Jacob and Coach Bramlet worked great together as coach and player, and Jacob was exposed to a lot of quality pitching time as a starter. Jacob brought valuable experience to the team from his various opportunities with Playball Baseball Academy and his collaboration with the Florida Bible's coach. Jacob was more experienced than the other pitchers on the team, and Coach Bramlet recognized that. Before graduating from East Coweta in 1996 Major League Baseball Draft was held, and the Montreal Expos selected Jacob to play pro baseball. After discussing his options with the Expos and carefully considering them, he decided to attend college and pursue his education while playing college baseball.

My First Day at Work

My first day at work was August 21, 1995, and I was assigned to work from 8:00 a.m. to 4:00 p.m. I spent that day meeting everyone and learning the locations of various office areas and airline offices. That first day was a lot to take in, as it involved learning about the people and the locations of the offices. I was starting a new position that I had never performed before.

Meeting the people and learning about the location was nice, but I was eager to begin my new Special Operations Inspector (SOI) role. I had a clear idea of the position, as I had read the description and made previous phone calls to the SOIs in Atlanta and other cities. I wanted to learn and understand everything I could about the position from different perspectives.

After speaking with everyone and researching the position, I realized it didn't adequately prepare me for what was to come.

After meeting

with the supervisors and speaking with Port Director Willie Anderson, I was given a few weeks to settle in, study how everything worked at the airport, and prepare cases for criminal prosecution because Assistant U.S. Attorneys (AUSA) work slightly differently in each state and location. I was accustomed to how the AUSA office in Miami worked, which had slightly different procedures than those in Atlanta. I immediately began learning about the types of international flights arriving each day. I pulled the reports and reviewed the past criminal and administrative cases that the SOIs had apprehended from those flights. I then studied the types of individuals who were apprehended, their criminal intent, and how the interviews of these individuals were conducted. I also checked the success rate when interviewing these individuals.

I was given an office, so on the second day, I settled in and unpacked the boxes I had previously sent from Miami. Of course, I asked Linda to come by and help me put everything in its right place. She came and put her decorative touch on everything, making my office the envy of all others.

SOI Duties

As the SOI, I was assigned to conduct secondary immigration inspections of individuals attempting to enter the United States suspected of engaging in fraud. I would interview these foreign nationals to assess their admissibility and, if necessary, gather evidence for a potential criminal prosecution case. I would encounter individuals pretending to be U.S. citizens, criminal aliens using fraudulent passports, or individuals who were previously deported and trying to return using fraudulent documents or documents belonging to another.

Working in Atlanta helped to expand my ability to conduct more interviews and improve my skills. Although I tried on many occasions to explain the reason behind my success, which was micro facial expressions, most other interviewers looked at me with a confused look, or they would lose interest as I tried to explain my techniques.

Assistant Port Director Stan Dedinas

Stan Dedinas was one of two Assistant Port Directors in Atlanta, and we became great friends. Stan was older than me, and he was my mentor because he was concerned about my career development. He always encouraged me to learn everything I could, increasing my chances of promotion when opportunities arose.

Stan had a liver transplant years before I arrived, and during my time in Atlanta, his liver began slowly deteriorating. After several years, the doctors advised him that he needed another transplant, and he was placed on a waiting list.

Months passed while Stan waited on a transplant list. He

carried a beeper and a cell phone that the hospital in New Orleans issued. He had to carry the two twenty-four hours a day to respond when alerted. Stan had previously arranged with Delta Airlines for when he received the phone call for the transplant, he would be on the first plane to New Orleans immediately, and Delta assured him they would be ready.

While at work, I would go into Stan's office every chance I could and talk with him. He was a walking textbook of immigration knowledge and a diplomat for the office, keeping peace between employees and the airlines. Whenever Willie had a problem with airline personnel, he would always ask Stan to defuse matters.

Stan had a soft-spoken voice and a warm fatherly smile. He had a way of making you realize that not everything was as bad as it seemed. He treated everyone as family, taking you for a walk to discuss issues or getting a soft drink or coffee if you were upset. He knew how to defuse any situation to make

everything good again. If he said he would do something for you, you could consider it done. He often told me that when dealing with people, "always keep your word."

One afternoon, he and I were working together when he got his phone call. We hurried to get Stan out of the office as he was calling his wife to come to the airport to meet him. As I told Stan goodbye and wished him good luck with his surgery, he hugged me and smiled, saying everything would be fine and he would see me soon.

That was the last time I saw my friend and mentor. The next day, I was notified that Stan didn't make it through the surgery and had died while on the operating table.

Stan's funeral was held on May 14, 1999, Chipley, Florida, and several of us from the office attended his funeral.

In the photo below, Linda, me, and Willie are third from left to right. Terry King, with red hair, is in the center, and Jan Eldridge is next to her. Jack Paul is standing far to the right at the end, and two inspectors are standing in the back.

Stan was a great man who helped me in so many ways. When I got aggravated at work, I often thought about how he would manage things.

It was several weeks after the funeral before Willie opened Stan's office just out of respect because Stan's death affected everyone at the airport, including the airline's personnel.

Firearms Instructor School

On Oct 17, 1995, I was asked to attend firearms instructor school at the Federal Law Enforcement Training Center in Glynco, GA. The school prepared me to be a firearms instructor, teaching others about the safety of weapons and how to improve their shooting skills.

Upon graduating, I returned to Atlanta as a firearms instructor, teaching employees how to use firearms responsibly and/or training them to use specific service weapons. I also assisted with firearms qualifications for all areas of responsibility at Atlanta Inspections.

On May 20th, I was tasked with taking over the firearms program and becoming the Firearms Instructor for the Atlanta District, which included inspectors from Atlanta, Wilmington, Charlotte, NC, and Charleston, SC.

On September 9, 1997, I attended another firearms instructor program in Watertown, NY, to become a firearms instructor for the new weapons assigned to the U.S. Immigration and Customs Enforcement's (ICE) inspection programs. Upon completion, the training enabled me to instruct employees in using the new service weapon (.40 cal. Beretta 96D) and perform modifications and repairs on weapons in the field. This would save time by eliminating the need to perform minor repairs in the office rather than sending the weapon to the National Firearms Center for repairs.

I conducted quarterly firearms qualifications for the Atlanta District Inspections program while using a government-issued Chevy van to load my ammunition, targets, and safety gear. I traveled to all the assigned offices to conduct the qualifications, and each office arranged a suitable location. I would stay overnight at each location before moving to my next office. I was later assigned to maintain qualifications for the entire

Atlanta firearms program, which includes the Inspections Program, Deportation Officers, Criminal Investigators, and Adjudication Examiners. I supervised two other firearm instructors and one range officer to help plan, organize, and schedule quarterly qualifications for over 160 employees.

1996 Atlanta Summer Olympics

Atlanta hosted the 1996 Summer Olympics, and I was appointed to oversee prosecuting immigration criminal cases presented before an Immigration Judge. I reviewed those cases for completion and ensured proper charges were applied for deportation proceedings.

I developed the "Fast Track Program for the Olympics," which I designed and presented to the port director for approval. After his approval, the proposal was forwarded to the Atlanta District Director for

Immigration, who also approved it. Part of the program required an immigration judge to be physically located at the Hartsfield International Airport so that violators attempting entry into the U.S. would be immediately presented to the judge to obtain deportation orders.

After the Olympics, I was recognized for my efforts because the Fast Track program was successful. It helped streamline the deportation process, save jail space in detention facilities, and significantly reduce the government's expenses.

On August 4, 1996, I received a signed certificate from the Immigration Commissioner for helping with the 1996 Atlanta Olympic Games.

CIA Training

On August 18, 1996, I was required to attend a conference on international terrorism at the Central Intelligence Agency (CIA) HQ in Langley, Virginia. There was so much activity occurring around the world, and terrorism was a high priority. The CIA HQ was an interesting place that featured memorials, art, museum galleries, and so much more. However, for security reasons, tours of the CIA HQ were not offered to the general public, and to enter the building, you had to possess a security clearance at the level of "Secret" or higher. At the time, I held a "Secret" clearance and had no issues entering the building for the conference. But even with a Secret clearance, you were not allowed to roam the building hallways without the escort of a person who held a "Top-Secret" clearance or higher. While attending the conference and needing to use the restroom, one of the agents with a Top Secret clearance escorted you. Those with Top-Secret clearance could roam about the building without escort, but if you had a Secret clearance and were walking the hallway alone, you were often challenged and asked to present your clearance credentials. You would then be escorted back to your conference or out of the building.

While attending the CIA training, I have two short stories to tell.

First, since I had a secret clearance, I could go to the dining hall for lunch, but I had to be mindful of where I sat. There were areas in the dining hall that were blocked off and designated for CIA employees who needed a private space to discuss work-related issues. This secure area was designed for complete privacy and featured soundproofing, ensuring no one could listen in on or intercept a conversation. There were also areas for employees to sit and have general discussions designed for minimal privacy.

I had lunch in the general population area, which lacked privacy, and I was not allowed to discuss casework with anyone. It was a monitored area, so I sat there, shutting my mouth, and ate lunch. I had a hamburger and fries, which were very good. Other individuals sat around me, engaging in small talk, but I remained silent, nodding and saying hello.

Secondly, one day during the conference, I wanted to call Linda to see how things were going back home. When we had our hourly break, I stepped out of the conference room and noticed a red phone booth with a phone positioned on each side. Several phone booths were in the hallway, and one was outside my conference room. I thought, how convenient. I had to figure out what it took to make the call because I would call Linda collect.

Sitting in the conference, I was getting excited because, during my next break, I would get to talk with Linda and check on everything at home. Additionally, I had a phone booth right outside the conference door, and I intended to use it.

Finally, my break time arrived. I left the conference room and walked to the red phone booth as planned. I opened the booth door, stepped inside, and picked up the phone receiver. The problem: I could not figure out how to call on it. As I stood there for several minutes trying to obtain a dial tone, someone from the agency noticed me in the booth. He was well dressed, in a suit and tie, and stepped over to me, knocking on the glass door. As I opened it, he asked me what I was doing. I explained that I wanted to make a phone call to my wife to check on her. He briefly chuckled and then explained how the booths worked. He said that agency employees use booths along the hallways for private conversations. They are secure phone booths and highly protected from any satellite

interference from foreign entities that may penetrate the building. He explained that two individuals would each enter one side of the booth, pick up the receivers, and dial their assigned badge numbers, connecting the two. They could have private conversations in the booth without any potential outside interference. Also, the conversations would be recorded for their files. Needless to say, I felt like an idiot, but he and I spoke for a while about how most things work around the building.

He told me he had been with the agency for the past eleven years and went on to explain some of the tricks people played on him when he was first hired. We laughed for a while, and he gave me his business card, saying, 'If you have any questions, please don't hesitate to call me.''

While there, I quickly learned much about the cloak-and-dagger CIA operations, but I didn't call Linda that day from the red phone booth. I patiently waited until I returned to my hotel, as I knew how to use the phone there.

On February 12, 1997, I had the opportunity to return to the CIA HQ for another conference on terrorism. This time, I had acquired my "Top-Secret" clearance, and I couldn't wait to check in and be able to walk those hallways as I damn well pleased.

I can assure you that I did not try to make any phone calls from those red phone booths. After the conference, I visited the CIA museum and toured the building. It was an interesting place, and I am glad I could see it all.

On October 20, 1997, I attended a week-long intelligence conference on Middle East terrorism in Virginia Beach, VA, promoted by the CIA and FBI. This conference was intense and covered a lot of vital information to absorb.

Senior Immigration Inspector

On January 19, 1997, I was selected to fill a Senior Immigration Inspector position in Atlanta. The port director requested that I return to the senior inspector program to oversee the criminal prosecutions from the airport.

As I previously explained regarding the senior inspector positions, conducting criminal investigations of individuals who violate INS laws and attempt to enter the U.S. was a priority. These cases were presented to the U.S. Attorney's Office for a grand jury hearing and criminal prosecution.

The Senior Inspector's duties in Atlanta were the same as when I worked in Miami, so it was all familiar to me, and I could step right into the position and perform the duties. I enjoyed working as a senior inspector because it allowed me to

get involved from the beginning of a case and work it through to prosecution if needed.

The special operations position allowed me to interview suspects frequently, and when I developed a case, it was referred to the senior program for prosecution.

As a Special Operations Inspector, you would interview one suspected violator after another while developing cases. Because you were so busy interviewing people, you never had the opportunity to pursue the prosecution side. The moment you finished one interview, you went straight to the next.

As a senior inspector, I presented the prosecution cases from the special operations inspectors. I was exceptionally skilled at conducting interviews, so I was allowed to participate in all cases and initiate the interview process. I could then follow it through to completion, which made me very happy.

Supervisory Immigration Inspector

One day, while at work, the port director and one of the assistant port directors approached me regarding the supervisory immigration inspector position that was becoming available. Both suggested I apply for the position because they felt working as a supervisor would prepare me for future promotions. I submitted my application after carefully considering and discussing the position with Linda.

On July 19, 1998, I was officially selected as a Supervisory Immigration Inspector in Atlanta, marking the beginning of the next chapter in my career.

As an Immigration supervisor, I oversaw the entire inspection program in Atlanta, making decisions on the admissibility of arriving passengers and preparing work schedules for inspectors while managing all immigration- related issues that arose at the airport. I also evaluated the work performance of all the immigration inspectors and issued yearly appraisals.

On several occasions, I was asked to serve as an acting Assistant Port Director for Atlanta. I received training in Immigration Quality Assurance classes, Workers' Compensation, Federal Labor Relations, dealing with Bargaining Unit Employees, and Ethical Conduct Standards.

In August 1996, I was sent to the Immigration Academy in Glynco to assist the federal firearms program in its training curriculum. Unfortunately, on August 19th, I injured my left knee while performing firearms tactical training techniques at the academy.

On September 9, 1998, after numerous surgeries to repair the knee, I had to undergo a total knee replacement. Luckily, I had a helpful nurse, Linda, who made the experience much easier.

My surgeon was Dr. Michael Gruber from Newnan, and the surgery was performed at the Newnan hospital. A funny story occurred before I had the surgery. Before knee replacement surgery, you must watch a video on what to expect before, during, and after the procedure.

Dr. Gruber's office arranged for me to pick up a VHS tape to watch, and then I could bring it back to the office. One afternoon, I went by the doctor's office and picked up the tape.

I brought it home, and Linda and I watched it. I put the tape in the VHS player, and it didn't take long before I realized it was not a tape about knee replacements because it was an adult porn movie.

The next day, I contacted the doctor's office and spoke with the ladies there about the tape. They asked me if I enjoyed it, and I explained that it wasn't about a knee replacement, but rather about things I already knew about. After a few questions from her, I told her it was an adult porn tape.

At first, she didn't believe me and thought I was joking. I took the tape to her, and it turned out that the two doctors in the office were playing a trick on each other by switching tapes in

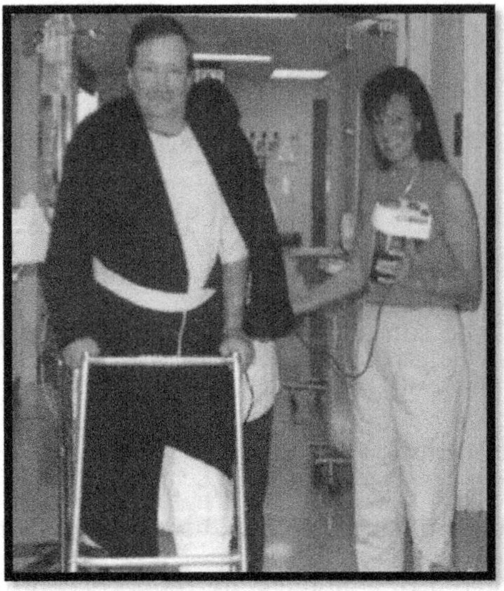

the boxes. They didn't realize the nurse would grab one of the tape boxes and give it to a patient to watch.

The entire office at Dr. Gruber's was embarrassed, and the doctors apologized numerous times while explaining the mix-up. I laughed it off, and they provided the genuine tape for me to watch. It all turned out well.

Middle Georgia Junior College

On May 13, 1996, Jacob was scheduled to try out at Middle George College, a two-year junior college in Cochran, GA. I drove him to the college, and he worked out as a pitcher for the head coach. Jacob pitched for a while, and then the coach walked over to me and said he wanted Jacob to attend school there, offering him a full scholarship.

After tryouts, the coach talked with Jacob and offered him a full scholarship if he attended Middle Georgia and played baseball. Jacob liked the college, and we discussed

the baseball program and attending school there. The coach made a great offer, and Jacob took it and played there.

Before graduating from East Coweta, the Montreal Expos drafted Jacob to play professional baseball. But after careful consideration, he decided to continue playing college baseball at Middle Georgia. Gaining more experience playing college ball would provide him with additional experience at another level, better preparing him for the pros. Plus, he would get a paid education while playing.

After graduating from East Coweta, we packed up Jacob

and moved him into a dorm room on campus. This was the first time he had ever moved out of the house to live elsewhere. It was hard for him, but it was even harder for his mom and me.

I recall the first time we brought Jacob to his dorm building to unload his belongings and then had to say goodbye. Although he was only two and a half hours away, it seemed further when we got home without him that day. Cochran is southeast of Newnan, traveling through Macon, GA. I don't remember how long this hug was in the picture, but it took a while—Mama had to let go of her baby! I admit that it took Linda and me quite some time to get over Jacob's not being around the house. Many days, I would sit in the bonus room at home, depressed, with nothing to do and no one to throw the baseball

That was a big adjustment, so I threw myself into my work at the airport and did my best to move on.

Jacob settled in well at college and had a good roommate in his dorm. I believe he did better than his mom and me, living away from home. Jacob also settled in with the baseball team, pitching two seasons for Middle Georgia and statically had two great seasons.

While playing baseball, he earned two years of college

academics for free. However, Middle Georgia was a two-year college, so he had to decide where his next opportunity would come from for school and baseball.

Columbus State University

After leaving Middle Georgia, Jacob had a tryout for the Columbus State University baseball team in Columbus, GA., which was a Division II school. After tryouts, the head coach offered him a complete scholarship to play baseball. After careful consideration and weighing all options, Jacob accepted the offer. Jacob played one season for Columbus and had an incredibly good season, but an opportunity came for him to play Division I baseball at Georgia State University in Atlanta. Coach Mike Hurst called me one afternoon and discussed Jacob and how well he was pitching at Columbus. Coach Hurst told me that if we could get Jacob into school there, he would offer him a full scholarship to play baseball. Jacob accepted the offer and applied to the school.

Georgia State University

In 1997, Jacob transferred from Columbus State University to Georgia State University for his senior year. Playing for Coach Hurst, Jacob had a good season and made many new friends. Jacob enjoyed attending Georgia State and got a free education to boot.

High School Baseball Coach

After Jacob had left for Middle Georgia College, I experienced severe baseball withdrawals because he was no longer there. After work, I would come home and sit. I missed not having him around to throw the baseball or just being at home. I had to do something to occupy my free time. I have given much thought to coaching somewhere or even becoming a high school umpire.

I became good friends with Coach Bramlet when Jacob was at East Coweta. After Jacob graduated, Coach Bramlet asked me if I would assist him with the baseball program. I agreed, but I first attended the State of Georgia High School Athletic Association (GHSAA) to obtain my high school coaching certificate and credentials. After six weeks of attending the course, I graduated on June 10, 1996, allowing me to coach at the high school level. I joined the baseball team and began assisting Coach Bramlet.

I enjoyed being involved and made friends with all the players. After the season, I helped several players obtain scholarships to several colleges. Being involved helped me adjust to the annoying silence around the house and the frequent boredom until Jacob came home and brought some of his friends to visit.

Area Port Director Position

While working as a supervisor in Atlanta, a position as Area Port Director became available, opening up opportunities for candidates to fill it. The position was in the U.S. Virgin Islands, specifically on the island of St. Thomas. One day, I was sitting in my office, reading the job requirements, when the port director, Willie, walked into my office. He told me about the position and said I would be perfect. Willie told me I would be selected if I put in for it. I gave it a lot of thought and spoke with Linda about it, as it would be a significant move and a change in position. But living in the Virgin Islands? We gave it a lot of consideration and decided to apply, so I submitted the required paperwork in abundance. Then, I stopped thinking about it and said it would be if it were meant to be.

On April 22, 2001, I received a phone call from the Deputy District Director of Immigration in San Juan, Puerto Rico. San Juan was the District Office for the U.S. Virgin Islands operations. He spoke about the events happening around St. Thomas and St. Croix airports and their entire crew's ship operations. I listened to him, wondering where the conversation was going. When he was done speaking, he asked me if I had any questions about working in the Virgin Islands. I told him no, but why was he asking? He said, "Oops, I forgot to ask you, do you want to be the new Area Port Director for the U.S. Virgin Islands? I said, "Yes, sir, I do." He said I should receive my official notification in a few days and welcomed me to the islands.

I accepted the position and prepared to transfer to St. Thomas, USVI. The Port Director, Willie Anderson, and the Assistant Port Directors were happy for me and offered their assistance if needed.

My Statue of Liberty

There was one co-worker and a close friend I worked with named Terry King, who was also an immigration supervisor at the airport. Terry and I talked about everything and everybody all the time. Terry had a small green statue of liberty that she kept on her desk, and every day that I worked, I would sneak into her office and "borrow" the statue to put on my desk. Later that day, she would walk by my office, see the statue, and retrieve it to put back on her desk. This continued for a year, but she never complained; instead, she would remove the statue from my desk and return it to her office. Sometimes, if I did it twice in one day, I could hear her shouting my name aloud when she discovered the statue missing from her desk. It became a well-known fact that I would retrieve the statue from Terry's desk whenever I could.

Another supervisor, Jeff Binns, took the statue for himself one day. Not knowing what Jeff had done, I went to Terry's office to get the statue, but it was not there. I thought Terry was hiding it from me, so I would patiently wait for her to return it. A brief time later, Terry came to me, wanting the statue back because she couldn't find it on my desk. I told her I didn't have it because I hadn't found it earlier. After convincing her I did not take the statue, we concluded that someone else was involved. Terry and I teamed up and started secretly monitoring the offices, looking around at everyone's desks, but we couldn't find it anywhere.

I noticed that whenever we walked toward Jeff, he would do his best to get away from us, and if we were walking in his direction, he would disappear. Finally, I caught Jeff and started talking with him, hitting him hard with questions about the statue, and he broke like a rotten tree branch. So, I made a deal with him that we would take the statue back to Terry's office when she was not around and put it back on her desk without her knowing. We pulled it off, and Terry later came to me mad as hell because she thought I had it all this time. I did my best to convince her I had not taken it, but knowing what I knew made me laugh, making things worse. At that time, Jeff came walking by, asking questions as if he didn't know what was happening and acting innocently.

While I was off work, several days later, Jeff told Terry what happened to the statue. When I returned to work, Jeff told me he had told her everything, so I would wait for Terry to come to me with some remorse, but she never did. Later that evening, I approached her and asked if there was anything she wanted to discuss with me. She said, "No," and walked away.

I was getting mad because Jeff had told her what had happened. Terry played this until we were ready to get off work, and she came to me, hugging me while I was laughing. She said she knew it all day but wanted to make me suffer a little.

With me leaving Atlanta, Terry and her husband wanted to meet Linda and me for our going-away dinner. We met at a restaurant, and when dinner was over, Terry reached down in a bag and gave me the Statue of Liberty. She said I possessed it as much as she had and wanted me to have it. I still have that statue in my study at home today, and every time I see it, I think about the fun we had with it.

Several years later, Terry was diagnosed with breast cancer, and she eventually passed away. I will forever keep that statue in memory of Terry.

Several weeks after our dinner with Terry, we packed and prepared to move to St. Thomas, U.S.V.I., and my new position.

On to St. Thomas, USVI.

Chapter 13

United States Virgin Islands (USVI)

After being notified of my selection to fill the Area Port Director (APD) position, I was contacted by U.S. Immigration and Naturalization Service, District Director (DD) Myrna Pere. She requested that I visit the District Office in San Juan, PR, to meet with her before entering duty. The District Office manages the Puerto Rico and the U.S. Virgin Islands offices.

On April 19, 2001, at 9:00 a.m., the moving packers arrived to pack up our home in Rayner Woods, preparing for our move to St. Thomas. The packers stayed all day and finished packing around 5:00 p.m.

On April 21st, the moving van arrived at 9:40 a.m., and they started loading our furniture onto the truck. This took all day and was completed around 5:00 p.m.

During the loading day, several neighbors came by to wish us well, even bringing us some gag gifts as a joke. We enjoyed all of our friends in the neighborhood, and it was sad to say goodbye. After the moving van and neighbors left, Linda and I spent our last night in the house, sleeping on the floor in the bonus room. Before going to St. Thomas, I have to fly to San Juan, PR, to meet with the District Director, Myrna Pere.

I flew out of Atlanta on April 22, 2001, arriving in San Juan at 3:30 p.m. I checked in at the Embassy Suites Hotel, which was located near the district office. After checking in, I rested most of the evening and had dinner at the hotel while preparing information for tomorrow's meeting with the directors.

Deputy District Director (DDD) Robert Bowles visited the hotel and escorted me to the district office the next day. I met the District Director and numerous other staff members and support personnel.

After spending most of the day at the district office, I had my last meeting with the DD and DDD. Both explained that about a year ago, the prior APD, along with several immigration inspectors in St. Thomas, were arrested for their involvement in a prostitution ring on the island. An immigration inspector working in St. Thomas had purchased a nude strip club, and he paid other immigration inspectors to illegally admit females from the Dominican Republic to dance at his club. This was done with the knowledge of the previous APD, who condoned the behavior and was paid for his silence. The DDD stated that he believed there were more immigration inspectors involved than just those arrested, and he asked me to keep an eye on the matter. The DD requested that, if possible, I rotate all the inspectors off the island to clean house and fill those positions with new inspectors for the inspections program. All employees working in the USVI are appointed for a three-year term, with the option to extend for an additional two years, resulting in a total of five years of appointment. However, some inspectors had been there for over five years and needed to be rotated back to the States.

(From the front row, I am third from the left, Commissioner of INS, DD Pere, and DDD Bowles)

After our meeting, I flew to St. Thomas from the airport, arriving at 5:09 p.m. Linda had traveled that day and was to arrive in St. Thomas close to my arrival time. I asked one of the immigration supervisors to meet and escort her to my office so she could wait for my arrival.

Linda was traveling with our cat Sam, "Sweet Baby," who was slightly medicated for the trip from Georgia, so I wanted Linda to have help getting to my new office. Before leaving Newnan, Linda visited a veterinarian and received medication to help Sam rest during the trip.

When Linda arrived at the office, poor Sam was still medicated and could barely stand up, falling off a table. Not long after Linda arrived, I arrived. I spoke briefly with some personnel and supervisors, but it was getting late, and we were exhausted. I picked up the keys to the government vehicle and took Linda and Sam to our assigned government apartment. The government had leased apartments at Sea Cliff Villas, near the airport, for all employees to live while working in St. Thomas. When we arrived at the apartments, we met the person who oversaw the apartments for the government, and we obtained the apartment keys.

Sea Cliff Villas

I took annual leave on the first day on the island to help Linda prepare the apartment for move-in.

We were assigned to building #22, apartment 24, so we cleaned the apartment before heading to a K-Mart store in the island's countryside for supplies. We arrived on the island during the start of the carnival season, which took place in downtown Charlotte Amalie.

(Above is Sea Cliff Villas)

The carnival takes place every year from April 27 to May 3. It features a J'ouvert waterfront street dance with bands on trucks, children's and adult parades with elaborate costumes, and various pageants. There is also a food fair and carnival village, where you can enjoy local cuisine, calypso, and reggae nights.

On Saturday, April 28, we went downtown to the carnival by calling a taxi to pick us up at the apartments, which cost us

$12. While there, we shopped at the events and watched the constant parades pass us. By 3:00 p.m., we were tired of all the walking and shopping, so we caught a taxi back to the apartments for another $12.

It was a fun day, and we soaked in the festival's ambiance while pointing out all the restaurants we wanted to try and the shops we wanted to visit. It took us time to realize that we live here now and could return to the shops and restaurants anytime.

While living in the US Virgin Islands, friends often asked about the need for passports and visas to visit us. The USVI is a group of Caribbean islands and an unincorporated and organized territory of the United States. As a result, a U.S. citizen does not need a passport to enter the USVI.

The USVI consists of the main islands of Saint Croix, Saint John, and Saint Thomas, with Charlotte Amalie serving as the capital of the islands on St. Thomas.

First Day at Work

On April 25, 2001, I reported to the Charlotte Amalie International Airport office. Still, I remember that morning, before leaving for work, we sat on the back patio overlooking the ocean and watched the cruise ships entering the seaport downtown.

I had my first staff meeting at 10:00 a.m. After that, I started preparing my office by unloading the boxes I had shipped and hanging a few things. But I kept getting interrupted by having to meet with representatives from other government agencies and get my bearings on where everything was located.

The next day, I conducted a meeting of Supervisory Immigration Inspectors in St. Thomas, where I met the supervisors one-on-one. The meetings went well; they addressed my questions and considered my ideas for possible changes.

I eventually met with the Senior Immigration Inspectors to discuss why they lacked criminal prosecutions. Their reports showed incredibly small numbers of criminal prosecutions. I know St. Thomas was a delightful place to work, but some form of criminal activity had to occur. Fortunately, after our meeting and over the next several weeks, the number of criminal arrests increased, and more prosecution cases were presented to the U.S. Attorney's Office. I noticed that even the administrative cases, such as deportation cases, at the airport have increased.

Before my arrival, I believed that everyone had become complacent in their work. They were able to get by or do as they pleased without supervision.

I spent time arranging my office and making it look more respectable, but I was not doing well. I called my interior decorator, Linda, to come by the office to bail me out. She put everything in its rightful place, making the office look much better than mine. On May 16th, our Mercury Sable arrived from the States, so we went to the seaport to pick it up. It was so good to have our own car, especially for Linda, because I had an assigned government vehicle

that Linda could not drive. Having our vehicle back gave Linda more freedom and the opportunity to go shopping.

As the Area Port Director, I supervised and was responsible for the U.S. Immigration offices on all three islands of St. Thomas, St. John, and St. Croix.

The offices on St. Thomas included airport immigration inspections, seaport inspections, crew ship operations, the Office of Investigations, the Office of Detention and Deportation, the Office of Adjudications, the Media Office, Congressional Inquiries, and Liaison with the Virgin Islands Governor's Office.

The island of St. John included two seaports and crew ship operations. It primarily used the Cruz Bay area for its seaport activities. I visited the St. John office weekly to review and support their progress.

St. John is nineteen square miles and has an approximate population of 4,500. It is the smallest of the three main U.S. Virgin Islands and about four miles east of St. Thomas.

The offices on St. Croix included airport immigration inspections, seaport inspections, crew ship operations, and the Office of Examinations. At least once a month, I traveled to St. Croix to inspect and support the offices. I would fly on Cape Air to visit the St. Croix office, spending a few days there each time.

St. Croix is the largest of the islands, with a population of approximately 41,000. Its nickname is "Twin City" for its two towns: Frederiksted on the western end and Christiansted on the northeast part of the island.

For the USVI, I was the first-line supervisor of five Supervisory Immigration Inspectors and four Senior Inspectors. Three immigration supervisors were located on St. Thomas, one supervisor was for Examinations, and one was at St. Croix inspections. There were three senior inspectors on St. Thomas and one on St. Croix.

I served as a second-line supervisor to over 150 personnel across various departments, including Inspections, Investigations, Adjudications, Deportation and Detention, Information Officers, and other support staff.

I managed all investigative activities and special operation cases assigned from the District Office in San Juan to the field offices. I supervised Special Agents (SAs) who conducted highly complex, challenging, and sensitive criminal investigations involving violations of U.S. immigration laws, regulations, and other federal statutes.

I supervised the administrative, logistics, budget, financial, and human resources management functions relative to the staff I supervised. I also established guidelines and performance expectations for all employees and staff members.

I observed employees' performance and provided constructive feedback when needed. I often counseled supervisors on work and administrative matters, including implementing appropriate disciplinary measures.

My main objective with the supervisors and seniors was to provide them with everything they needed to accomplish their goals. In turn, they would provide for the employees they supervised and assisted.

(St. Thomas cruise ship operations)

During my tenure, up to seven cruise ships docked at one time in St. Thomas. On the other side of the island, another seaport permitted two more cruise ships to dock.

St. Thomas was the premier port of call for cruise lines in the Virgin Islands, boasting two well-equipped docks: the West Indian Co. Dock (WICO) and Crown Bay Dock (CB). Ships could also anchor within the Charlotte Amalie harbor when needed.

The cruise ships docking in St. Croix would do so at the

Frederiksted Pier, while those anchoring in St. John would do so at Cruz Bay.

Some days at work were more difficult than others. There were days when all you had to deal with were issues related to airport inspections, but then there were days when every office had problems, and I had to get involved.

As the Area Port Director, I attended extensive training and flew to San Juan every other week. I used Cape Air, a six-seater plane. There was only one pilot, so I would fly most of the time in the co-pilot seat for weight distribution. A seaplane operated out of St. Thomas, and I frequently used it to fly to San Juan and St. Croix.

Traveling between the islands of St. Thomas and St. John was also easy on a ferry. A public ferry service between St. Thomas and St. John ran daily. They link the ferry terminal at Red Hook, on the East End of St. Thomas, with Cruz Bay in St. John.

Riding each way was a small cost, but I don't remember the exact price from 2001. As the Area Port Director, they never charged immigration for travel.

Every day on the islands brought new adventures because something was always happening, was about to happen, or had already happened. When I thought I had a handle on everything for the day, something else would happen.

Training was constant for me because immigration laws were changing and redefining how we conducted business. When I returned from one training session, they would send me off the island for training elsewhere.

On July 9, 2001, I was sent to Burlington, VT., to a Port Director's conference, which lasted three days. While away, I worried about what was happening back on the islands. When I returned home, I found everything in working order and no fires to put out. All the offices were in line with their responsibilities, and the seaports and cruise ship operations ran smoothly. I was proud of how everything was shaping up on the islands, considering all the issues they had experienced before I arrived. I felt like I was making a positive difference, and everything turned around for the better.

The Baths

I worked hard, but I also took time to enjoy myself and go touring the British Virgin Islands. One place we enjoyed was "The Baths" at Virgin Gorda, British Virgin Islands. The Baths featured boulders and caverns that formed a maze leading to secret rock pools and the famous Cathedral Room, a natural pool located within a small cave.

You can go to the beach at Devil's Bay to swim, snorkel, and take in the view from the Top of the Baths restaurant.

Magen's Bay

On St. Thomas, we had several places to relax and escape from work. I was always working, and Linda was busy getting the apartment together and shopping for groceries. A good friend told us about Magen's Bay, where we could relax and have a great time.

Magen's Bay was a horseshoe-shaped tropical beach, perfect for relaxation, with water sports, sunbathing, and many people picnicking.

Linda was always working on her tan, so I would walk along the beach, taking in the views.

Magen's Bay was also a popular port of call for cruises and a frequent stop on island tours. On some days, it was busy with tourists. We sought peace and privacy, so we occasionally visited on weekdays, avoiding the crowds of tourists. If you drove up to the "Mountain Top lookout," the views were breathtaking.

Not long after arriving on the island, I felt the urge to dive into the beautiful blue waters. One problem was that I did not know how to dive, so I had to take diving lessons. At first, Linda wanted to dive, but when it came to taking the classes, she decided she would be a snorkeler instead. I arranged my diving lessons with Chris Sauer Dive Center and eventually completed the course, earning my certificate.

Scuba diving in the Virgin Islands was great because, in most places you dove, there were large schools of tropical fish and numerous reefs, and some locations featured old shipwrecks to explore.

I often saw lobsters, turtles, moray eels, groupers, and nurse sharks that would swim right next to you, allowing you to touch them as they passed.

There was a time when I dove so much during the week that

the diving shops restricted my diving and made me wait a few days for safety reasons. This happened several times, giving me an idea: Why not buy my diving gear? I visited my favorite diving shop, purchased the tank and all the necessary gear to dive independently, and got myself set up!

I loved diving so much that on my birthday, Linda gave me a dive watch that I used while diving. I still have that watch and wear it occasionally.

Linda and I also like snorkeling, and we often do that in numerous places. Since Linda loved to snorkel, I asked one of the dive instructors to take us on a night snorkel. Unlike

Snorkeling during the day is a unique experience, but after it gets dark, you experience many nocturnal things that you would not do during the day. Snorkeling at night is a whole new experience.

Our guide explained that the ocean becomes more scenic at night since most marine life and creatures become active. Coral opens, and some rare sea creatures emerge, allowing you to see things you would otherwise not see during the day. The experience of darkness can be nerve-wracking, especially if you are not used to snorkeling.

We had to use several essentials: a waterproof flashlight and a whistle, which we tied around our necks in case we needed to signal each other. The flashlight illuminated the ocean floor, allowing us to see the surroundings. It will let you see things you would not otherwise be able to experience in daylight.

Linda had made many friends in St. Thomas, but one person with whom she became good friends was Maria Montalvo, an Immigration Inspector at the airport. Those two would go anywhere and were not afraid of anything.

One amusing story I must share about them is that one day, while I was working, they decided to take a day trip to Tortola, British Virgin Islands, departing from the St. Thomas waterfront. They had left their vehicle parked at the waterfront so they would have it upon their return. They spent the day in Tortola, and that afternoon, when they attempted to catch the ferry back to the waterfront, it broke down and was out of service. The only way for them to return to St. Thomas was to catch the ferry boat, which leaves Tortola and goes to Red Hook in St. John.

They tried to call me from Tortola, but they forgot that they had no service due to the international time difference. They caught the ferry boat back to Red Hook, and when they arrived, they could call me. However, I was worried because I had not heard from them all day.

It was evening when I finally received their phone call. Linda explained why they had to come into Red Hook and asked if I would pick them up. Linda later told me that Maria was so worried that I would be mad about having to come pick them up, but I wasn't. When I arrived to pick them up, I made them wait and bought myself dinner, consisting of beer and wings.

September 11th

On September 11, 2001, I was attending a conference in Dallas, and Linda was in Atlanta visiting Jacob when the World Trade Center was attacked. The airlines immediately shut down, and I could not fly out of Dallas to meet Linda in Georgia. A few people at the conference drove their vehicles and could drive home. Those who flew were waiting to see what would happen with the airlines. Since most of us were stuck in Dallas, the conference continued.

I befriended one person from Atlanta who had leased a vehicle and drove home at the end of the conference. He invited me to ride with him, and I accepted his offer. We drove straight to Atlanta, and I met Linda at Jacob's house.

On October 15th, I booked a flight from Atlanta and returned to St. Thomas, as I needed to resume work. Linda flew back several days later, and I was glad when we were reunited and could stay together.

Hershel Miller

One of my supervisors had recently transferred from St. Thomas to Calgary, Canada, to work as a supervisor for U.S. Immigration, overseeing pre-clearance inspections. I announced his position to fill it, and after announcing the job, I received a phone call from a friend I worked with in Minneapolis, Mike Conway. Mike was now working in Kentucky as the Director of Examinations for Immigration. Mike saw the announcement and asked me to review the application of his friend, Hershel Miller, who was living in Hawaii but also had a residence in Kentucky. Mike said Hershel had recently retired from immigration while in Hawaii and decided to return to work. Mike informed me that he and Hershel were friends, having known each other for a long time. Hershel was seeking a supervisory position with immigration in the Caribbean islands, so since I had an opening in St. Thomas, he thought Hershel would be a good fit for my office. When the list of candidates for the supervisory position was announced, Hershel's name was at the top as the most qualified. I phoned Hershel, and we talked for a long time, and I liked him from the start. Hershel would bring a lot of supervisory experience, and he displayed a calming demeanor that was desperately needed. I selected Hershel for the position, and in November 2001, he was on-site, ready to take on the role.

Hershel was a kind man, and everybody was happy when he arrived. He knew how to talk with people and displayed that calming effect. It did not take long before Hershel became my point of reference, and I counted on him for everything. Everyone who met him respected his demeanor, and he became my best supervisor.

Hershel could see what was coming at us ahead of time, and I no longer had to look over my shoulder constantly. I often left Hershel in charge, and I didn't have to worry about anything. Of course, the other supervisors became jealous of the reaction Hershel was receiving from employees, but they knew they could not be as effective as Hershel.

Later, when I transferred from St. Thomas, I recommended that Hershel take over as the Area Port Director for the USVI

to the DD and DDD. Luckily, the DD had already noticed Hershel's work performance and had decided that he would be my replacement. Hershel made an excellent Area Port Director for the USVI and an asset to the government.

Hershel was later diagnosed with cancer and eventually passed away. He was a big man with a big heart who loved people and life. I was thankful that Mike called me that day and introduced me to Hershel; if not, I would have never had the opportunity to meet such a good man.

Liaison

On June 23, 2001, Charles W. Turnbull, Governor of the U.S. Virgin Islands, invited me to a luncheon at the Marriott. During lunch, Linda and I met many dignitaries and had the opportunity to speak with the governor for a brief period. We also met the Governor of the British Virgin Islands.

Governor Turnbull was first elected in 1999 and served two full terms as governor. He could not run for reelection in 2006 because he was subject to term limits. Governor Turnbull was diagnosed with cancer and died while living in

Washington, D.C., on July 3, 2022, at eighty-seven. Governor Turnbull was a large man with gigantic hands to shake.

I was constantly putting out fires from congressional inquiries in the liaison department. Some inquiries involved a U.S. citizens or foreign nationals complain to a congressional representative about how they were treated when attempting to enter the United States or being denied entry and subsequently returned to their country. Either way, my job was to put the fire out and make everything disappear.

The Representative for the USVI was Donna Christensen, who served from 1997 to 2014.

Rep. Christensen would contact me to assist her with diplomatic efforts for individuals who needed to come to the U.S. in an emergency and did not have time to obtain a visa or go through the State Department for relief. I would normally do my best to assist her and parole these individuals for the period they needed to accomplish their tasks.

Rep. Christensen was grateful for my assistance with these issues, and she always did her best to ensure that the immigration office for the USVI was taken care of by assisting with funding for training and/or equipment. Rep. Christensen and I had an outstanding working relationship, as evidenced by the letters of commendation she had written to me.

Sometimes, celebrities arrived in St. Thomas, passing through on their way to another destination, and sometimes, they stayed on a boat for a week or so.

(Pictured is Me and Chuck Norris.)

One morning, I received a call stating that Chuck Norris was returning from the West Indies and would be making an entry through St. Thomas. These notifications informed us that they would require special attention and that we should prevent other passengers from harassing them for autographs or pictures. I did what I could to assist their request.

On this occasion, I walked out to meet Chuck at his flight, and he had an hour before his connecting flight. He asked me if we could go somewhere and sit quietly, so I took him to my office, where we stayed until he was ready to depart. I conducted his inspection myself. We talked briefly in my office, and he also made some phone calls. However, when he was ready to leave, he asked me if I would take a photo with him, and I said, "Sure." I have a copy of that photo displayed at home.

It was sometime in November when I received a phone call from someone claiming to be Kurt Russell, stating that he was on a boat heading into the harbor of St. Thomas and requesting an immigration inspection upon arrival. I first thought it was a joke, but when he explained who was on the boat with him and that they had filled out the necessary documentation for entry, I started to believe him. I told him I would come to do the inspection myself, and when I arrived at the seaport, a small tender was waiting to pick me up. The man introduced himself as one of the crewmembers on Russell's boat, and he shuttled me out to the boat. The boat was a fifty-five-foot yacht, and when I boarded, Kurt Russell was waiting for me, holding a beer. Russell said he was in no hurry and asked me to sit and drink a beer with him. We talked for about fifteen minutes before Goldie Hawn stepped out of the cabin and walked toward me. As I stood up to shake her hand, she reached out and gave me a big hug. She sat with us, and we began discussing the virgin island.

I couldn't resist any longer and asked them about the movie Overboard. Both of them started laughing and telling me about making the film. It didn't take long before they began to accuse each other of lying about their story, and it was amusing to hear them share the story behind their movie. We sat for over an hour talking, and it was a lot of fun because they were common, ordinary people just out having fun. They did have one bodyguard on board, and he sat silently, but it was sometimes nice to laugh with us.

I completed the inspection and was leaving when Goldie said she was going shopping tomorrow morning and asked if I could meet her and show her where to go. I said I would and asked her to call me when she was ready.

The next morning, I received a call from Kurt, telling me that

Goldie would be at the seaport and asking me to look after her. When I arrived, I did not recognize her because she was dressed up like a tourist so that no one would recognize her. When

I met her, and she asked me if Linda would come and meet her to take her around so I wouldn't have to babysit her. I tried numerous times to contact Linda, but she was out jogging and missed the calls to meet with Goldie.

Later that day, Goldie returned to the boat, and they spent the next two days relaxing just off the coast. They asked me if I would help them to the airport when they were ready to leave, as they would be flying out of St. Thomas, while the others would take the boat back to Miami. They had leased the boat in Miami and traveled around the Caribbean before coming to St. Thomas.

A few days later, Kurt called again and asked if I could pick them up at the seaport. I took them to the airport and walked them through the clearance process to board their flight. It was fun meeting them and talking on their boat.

Conducting immigration inspections on cruise ships was unique. On one occasion, I was supervising the inspections when I noticed a man and his family standing in line waiting to be inspected by an immigration officer. Still, other passengers were crowding him and his family. People were trying to talk with him, and I could tell the man was becoming annoyed, so I walked over to him.

He immediately identified himself as Chris Dodd, a Senator from Connecticut. I asked him and his family to follow me and took them to the inspection area, where I completed their

immigration inspection myself. I then walked them out to the exit, where they could depart the ship to tour the island. Senator Dodd was so appreciative that he took the time to write me a note thanking me for my help and mailed it to me from Washington.

Working on cruise ships was enjoyable because you met a diverse range of people from around the world who came to the Islands. I was nice to everyone, helped people when needed, and did my best to relay that to the other inspectors.

St. John

My office in St. John remained busy daily, as the seaport there welcomed tourists from cruise ships and islanders who traveled back and forth between the British Virgin Islands (BVI). Many boats returning from fishing entered the BVI and were heading home to St. John or St. Thomas, but all had to be inspected by immigration and readmitted into the United States.

With cruise ships arriving daily and anchoring in the bay,

tourists were taken on tenders from the ships and transported to the immigration office for inspection. These cruise ship inspections went quickly, and passengers were allowed to visit the islands.

Kentucky Colonel

In 2002, I was nominated and became a Kentucky Colonel by Governor Paul Patton, who presented me with my certificate. The commission of the Kentucky Colonel is the highest honor bestowed by the Governor of Kentucky on an individual. It recognizes an individual's noteworthy accomplishments and outstanding service to the community, state, and nation. In a letter to the Kentucky Colonels, a sitting Kentucky governor noted that he commissioned individuals as Kentucky Colonels, "is a Governor's way of recognizing individuals for their service and accomplishments on behalf of others." If you are a commissioned Colonel, you are a Kentucky Colonel for life.

A Kentucky Colonel Commission is awarded in the name of the Commonwealth by the governor of Kentucky to individuals with "Honorable" titular style recognition preceding the names of civilians' noteworthy accomplishments, contributions to civil society, remarkable deeds, or outstanding service to the community, state, or nation. The Governor bestows the honorable title with a colonelcy commission by issuance of letters patent.

Many famous and noteworthy people have received commissions as Kentucky colonels. The award is equally available to individuals of all backgrounds, based on their accomplishments. A Kentucky Colonel is considered a goodwill ambassador of the State of Kentucky, its culture, traditions, and values. My Kentucky Colonel Certificate hangs in my study to this day.

Barb and Henry Vogel

Barb and Henry lived in the Thousand Islands, NY, but they would spend the winter in St. Thomas. We got to know them while hanging out by the apartment pool and spent much time together. Usually, we would go out to dinner somewhere on the weekends or hang out by the pool. Henry made his money over the years by restoring old vintage vehicles for resale, and

eventually, he established a dealership to sell them. Henry, The photo includes Linda, me, Barb, Eileen, and Steve. Steve and Eileen were also snowbirds from Boston, and they would come for the winter months like the Vogels.

Henry had a nice boat, and we were always on board whenever he took it out. It would not take much for Henry to call me during the week and say, "Let's take the boat out." We would take his boat somewhere/anywhere and drop an anchor to sit. Sometimes, I would bring my diving gear and dive while Linda snorkeled. Henry and Barb would swim, but most of the time, we would all sit around and relax. During times like that, it was nice to get away and relax. We enjoyed swimming in the warm waters, which stay around 80°F most of the year, or sunbathing on one of the beaches. After enjoying the sun, we often dine at one of the many restaurants offering traditional Virgin Islands cuisine. Over time, we learned to slow down our pace and acclimate to island life.

Anegada

Anegada is the northernmost of the British Virgin Islands. It is approximately fifteen miles north of Virgin Gorda and is the only inhabited British Virgin Island formed from coral and limestone. While other islands are mountainous, Anegada is flat, and its highest point is twenty-eight feet above sea level, approximately fifteen square miles.

You can access the island via the small Auguste George

Airport, a weekly ferry, or by private boat. We arrived by private boat with Henry as our Captain. We stayed at the Anegada Reef Hotel without a phone or TV. When we arrived, they asked us what we would like for dinner, and we had the option of lobster, fish, or steak. Everyone in our group selected Lobster, and dinner was served at a particular time when everyone came to the table together.

You could rent a small pick-up truck to drive around the island. We drove the truck to different beaches and then headed inland, where we found houses. We also went swimming and spent most of the day relaxing in the sun.

The next day, we left the island to return to St. Thomas, but the water was choppy on the way home, causing a rough ride. When we returned, everyone was exhausted and glad to be home.

Barb and Henry had a friend on the island who owned a catamaran and ran a charter service. The service took people on tours around the Bay of St. Thomas and the surrounding areas. People paid good money for the private tour and the opportunity to see things from the boat.

One evening, St. Thomas had a fireworks display downtown near the waterfront. Henry planned with his friend to take us on the catamaran to the bay so we could watch the fireworks that night. After dark, we took the catamaran to the bay to watch the fireworks. We got set up and enjoyed ourselves while waiting for the fireworks to start; however, when the fireworks finally began, we realized that we had gotten too close to the bay because the fireworks exploded directly over us, causing debris to fall all around our boat. We had to back the boat out of the bay to see and enjoy the display without injury. We laughed and had a great time that night, enjoying the evening.

Cleaning House

While in the USVI, I transferred over fifty inspectors, investigators, examiners, and clerical staff from the three islands and hired new employees to replace them. Others requested transfers independently, and employees asked for internal transfers for many reasons. The most common desire was to step into a new role superior to their current position, such as applying for promotions in other geographical locations.

Other reasons employees requested a transfer, in addition to seeking personal growth, included a better work-life balance. Some female employees sought a workplace that better accommodated their family lifestyle, allowing them to spend more time with their families.

Employees may need to change to benefit their mental or physical health. Their current position, which was highly demanding and required frequent overtime, significantly impacted their personal lives and well-being. They wanted to stay with the government but took on a less intense role that would allow them time to care for themselves or their family members. Some had been on the island longer than their required time allowed, and needed a change.

As I stated at the beginning of this chapter, any employee who transferred to the USVI was given a three-year assignment, with the possibility of two one-year extensions, allowing them five years to work in that position. Sometimes, employees become lost in the government's red tape after the five-year period expires. Employees with no issues at work may get overlooked, as they are often out of sight and out of mind.

When I arrived, I reviewed the records of all employees who had been with the company for over five years and called them in for an interview. I advised them that their time on the island was up, so they needed to decide which city to transfer to next. I gave each employee a week to decide, and most would have a town they would like to transfer to, so I would call the port director at that location and attempt to arrange their transfer. However, several employees refused to select a city or location, so I made that decision for them and sent them to locations that needed help.

It was good for all three islands to have new employees rotating in with fresh work ethics, ideas, and enthusiasm. New employees made life a little easier for the supervisors by eliminating the complaints and sarcastic remarks from employees.

When the employees on the islands realized I meant business and would transfer you off the island, their attitudes changed dramatically as all the new employees started arriving for work. Again, they now understood I was serious, and no one was indispensable.

Decision Making

When I arrived on the island, decision-making was viewed as a problem-solving activity to provide an optimal or satisfactory solution. My arrival meant that I had to make all the decisions that had been put on hold.

Most of my decision-making process involved finding the best alternative or solutions to existing problems.

I devised a solution for every issue I faced, presented it to the supervisors for their opinions, and even encouraged their

input. Once this was completed and we had a solution we could live with as supervisors, I brought it to the rest of the employees to hear their input. Once this was completed, I implemented the solution into daily business operations. By doing things this way, when all was said and done, no one could complain because everyone had an input.

New Orleans

Working at USVI was exciting, fun, and a terrific learning experience. Supervising so many departments allowed me to learn new things and generate innovative ideas for accomplishing goals.

While there, I encountered numerous experiences that helped me fully understand my mission with each department. These experiences taught me valuable lessons and equipped me with the tools to navigate the job's complexities. When the Supervisory Special Agent position became available in New Orleans, I considered putting in for the position. After some thought and discussion with Linda, I submitted my request for the position.

The employees at USVI threw me a going-away party with cake and gifts. I told them how much I would miss them and living the life on the island.

In June 2002, I transferred from St. Thomas after being selected as the Supervisory Special Agent for investigations in New Orleans.

Off to New Orleans!

Chapter 14

New Orleans Criminal Investigations

On May 30, 2002, I received official orders transferring me from the USVI to the Immigration and Naturalization Service (INS), Investigations, New Orleans, Louisiana District Office as a Supervisory Special Agent.

After receiving my notification, we planned for the movers to come and box our belongings at our apartment. I also arranged for our vehicle to be shipped back to New Orleans.

On June 13, 2002, Linda, Sam, and I left the USVI and flew to New Orleans to start a new phase. We arrived in New Orleans, and after retrieving our luggage from baggage claim, we rode the shuttle bus from the airport to the rental car office. We had to rent a vehicle because our vehicle was being shipped from the US Virgin Islands. We were thrilled and ready to return to the Amite area. We loaded the rental car with our luggage and headed down the interstate to Amite. We were close to arriving there when we realized we were missing one of our bags. The bag contained our jewelry, money, insurance papers, and much more, which we had kept in a safe deposit box in VI. I immediately got on my phone and called the car rental office. I told the gentlemen I had left a piece of luggage there and was headed back to retrieve it. I described it to him and asked him to hold on to it for us.

Arriving at the car rental office, the bag was waiting for us. We were in such a hurry to leave that we forgot our bags on the shuttle bus when we arrived at the car rental. The bus driver discovered them on the bus and dropped them off at the car rental office. Checking the bag, we found everything was secure and nothing was missing, so we were so blessed that day! One thing is certain: We have not forgotten our sweet baby girl, Sam!

Arriving in Amite, we arranged to temporarily stay at an apartment complex on North Duncan Avenue owned by our friends Chuck and Mary Ellen Brister. We knew Brister's before we left Amite to go to work for the government. We stayed there for a few months while deciding where to live and build a home. We had also previously purchased an acre of property in Clemons Court, located off North Duncan Avenue. However, we were still undecided about whether this was where we wanted to build our new home, so we explored other options.

On June 18, 2002, we purchased a home at 708 Courtney Drive in Tycer Park, Amite, until we could build our new home on the lot we owned at 1405 Clemons Court. We didn't know how long it would take to build, so the house on Courtney worked out for us, with plenty of room while we waited. We knew this house was not where we wanted to live permanently and that we would eventually sell it once our new home was completed.

After searching around, we decided to build our new home in Amite because Linda's mom, D-Dot, lived here, and she was getting older, so we thought it would be best to stay close to her in Amite.

We eventually chose a contractor to build our home, knowing it would take approximately six months to complete. Linda had previously purchased house plans for a Victorian home that she kept for several years; we used those plans to build our home.

We felt like we were back home now, and Linda would finally get to create the house she wanted —a Victorian-style home.

Our vehicle arrived from the USVI on June 24 in New Orleans, so we picked it up, returned the rental, and brought it home. It was nice to have our vehicle back safe and sound from the Islands.

Finally, on July 15th, our furniture arrived from the USVI and was delivered to the Courtney Drive address for now.

With this government-paid move, Linda no longer had to worry about Jacob's school system or learn where grocery stores were located, as she already knew where everything was in their small hometown. The move from USVI to New Orleans was the easiest and smoothest of our previous government moves. Everything went great, and we had no significant complications, except for leaving a bag of valuables at the airport.

After months of waiting and watching our contractor, Linda's new Victorian home was finally completed, and on August 15, 2003, we moved in enthusiastically. Our new home looked great and was everything Linda wanted in a house. It was a Victorian home with plenty of space for us, and even Sam liked it, too. Over time, Linda worked hard to decorate each room perfectly, achieving a subtle Victorian look. You could have the entire house photographed and displayed in Southern Living Magazine when she was done decorating. The bedrooms, kitchen, and bathrooms all had a Southern Living feel in a Victorian environment. People often would tour our master bedroom and ask Linda if I slept there.

We eventually sold our house on Courtney Drive, and it didn't take long before someone expressed interest in purchasing it when we were ready to sell.

My First Day at Work

I had to go to work sometime, so my first day was on July 1, 2002, as a Supervisory Special Agent (SSA). After meeting with the District Director of Investigations, I supervised a group of special agents (SA) assigned to the general criminal investigations section.

Special Agents rarely receive any form of overtime. As an SA, you are exempt from the Fair Labor Standards Act provisions; instead, SAs receive Law Enforcement Availability Pay, or

LEAP. This represents an additional 25% added to your base pay, averaging ten (10) work hours per day. Anything beyond 10 hours, you have essentially donated your time and workload to the government.

Arresting individuals was part of the job, and the same applied to executing arrest warrants and serving search warrants. On any given day, you may encounter someone trying to kill or harm you, and you are more likely to experience a confrontation with those you are trying to arrest. While conducting an arrest or search warrant, you have support from SAs who will offer assistance. Suppose the subject you are after is high-risk, such as someone with a significant criminal history, known for violence, and using firearms. In that case, you will likely use a team before entering a residence or business. Even then, you will have many other agents with you, and every contingency will be considered before entry.

Special Agent General Duties

The Department of Homeland Security Investigations (HSI) outlined the duties, responsibilities, work environment, and investigative authority. For example, an HSI special agent primarily investigates federal violations involving immigration, customs, human trafficking, narcotics, terrorism, general crime, and counterintelligence and can expect to be deployed anywhere in the world.

Special Agents are trained in various skills, including firearms training, defensive tactics training, physical restraint techniques, crime scene processing, suspect interviewing, protective service details, and specialized driving techniques. Staying in decent shape and maintaining functional fitness are significant in many of these tasks and should not be forgotten. Special agents can conduct undercover operations, execute arrest warrants, search warrants, surveillance, and wiretaps, deploy on an aircraft carrier, work with special forces, be assigned to an embassy, and become members of a SWAT team.

Criminal Alien Program (CAP)

Eventually, I was assigned to supervise CAP, and my group was responsible for covering the states of Louisiana, Arkansas, Mississippi, Tennessee, and Alabama, which were our areas of responsibility (AOR).

CAP consisted of six SAs and me. We initiated removal proceedings (deportation) against criminal aliens, worked closely with state and local law enforcement agencies, and reviewed all jails and prisons within our Area of Responsibility (AOR).

CAP identified incarcerated noncitizens and initiated deportation proceedings against them to deport them from the

United States. This meant conducting extensive interviews with these individuals to determine their deportability. We investigated these individuals and prosecuted them for any immigration violations in conjunction with the U.S. Attorney's Office.

We also investigated and arrested individuals who were in the U.S. illegally. We identify, investigate, and arrest at-large "criminal aliens" convicted of drug trafficking offenses, crimes of violence, sex offenses, human trafficking, and smuggling offenses.

As the Supervisory Special Agent, I managed the office by reviewing investigative reports, overseeing the progress of criminal cases, and arranging financial budgets for investigations. I also updated my agents on travel status and performed case management reviews. Running the CAP unit involved significant work; however, all assigned agents had the necessary experience and required minimal supervision.

Working in CAP was sometimes exciting. I hunted down criminal aliens running from law enforcement and interviewed them. CAP was the place to learn interview techniques and build criminal prosecution cases.

Regarding September 11, 2002 (911)

The Federal Government Historical Archives provided the

information below. This occurred while I was assigned to New Orleans Criminal Investigations.

A significant change occurred on March 1, 2003, that realigned federal government agencies. Before March 1, 2003,

the U.S. Immigration and Naturalization Service (INS) was an agency of the U.S. Department of Justice (DOJ) from 1940 to 2003. It was known as INS, but the agency ceased to exist under that name on March 1, 2003, when most of its functions were transferred to three new entities – U.S. Citizenship and Immigration Services (USCIS), U.S. Immigration and Customs Enforcement (ICE), and U.S. Customs and Border Protection (CBP) – within the newly created U.S. Department of Homeland Security (DHS), as part of a major government reorganization following the attacks on September 11, 2001.

In March 2003, the administration over immigration services, including permanent residence, naturalization, asylum, and other functions, became the responsibility of the United States Citizenship and Immigration Services (USCIS).

The INS's investigative and enforcement functions, including investigations, deportation, and intelligence, were combined with those of U.S. Customs investigators to create

U.S. Immigration and Customs Enforcement (ICE).

The INS's border functions, which included the Border Patrol and INS Inspectors, were combined with U.S. Customs Inspectors to create U.S. Customs and Border Protection (CBP).

As of March 1, 2003, all U.S. Immigration Inspectors fell under the jurisdiction of CBP, and the investigations branches of INS and U.S. Customs were combined to form ICE. In March 2003, I became an employee of ICE, which was then under the Department of Homeland Security (DHS).

The change was a title change, and all the laws remained the same. U.S. Customs investigators joined us from INS investigations, and we shared the load of the legacy INS laws and the U.S. Customs laws.

Training

In August 2003, I attended a weeklong DHS undercover school in Potomac, MD. The course instructed on effective recruitment and utilization of informants, identifying safety considerations, and unique problems associated with undercover work. It addressed the psychological challenges of undercover work, identifying difficult undercover situations and demonstrating methods to resolve them. We discussed prosecutorial guidelines, regulations, and entrapment issues while discussing risk management for undercover operations. We also discussed key issues in supervising undercover units and personnel. The course was highly informative, covering a lot of material in just one week.

While there, several of us in the class wanted to see the New York Yankees vs. the Baltimore Orioles baseball game. We were able to leave class early one afternoon to attend the game.

Training was necessary in the CAP because policy and procedures changed for the government, local jails, and state prisons. We had to stay updated with the latest interview and interrogation techniques and all the changes involving immigration laws. Training was a constant for me and the agents in my unit.

Hurricane Katrina

On August 26, 2005, we learned that Katrina's potential path was headed directly to New Orleans. This scenario was considered a potential catastrophe because some parts of New Orleans and its surrounding metro area are located below sea level. On August 28, Katrina was a Category 5 storm and was headed straight for

the New Orleans area. On August 29, Katrina came ashore and struck us hard.

The eye of Hurricane Katrina made landfall near Buras in Plaquemines Parish at approximately 6:00 a.m. as a Category 3 hurricane with maximum winds at 125 miles per hour to the east of its center. Shortly before landfall, Katrina was moving at 12 mph, a relatively slow speed for a hurricane. A slow-moving storm can be more destructive than one that moves quickly.

In Amite, we were without power for several weeks, but we could still cook our meals on our natural gas grill in the backyard. We had no cell phone communication for a long time, but eventually, everything returned to normal. Power was restored, cell service resumed, and stores reopened for shopping.

Becoming a Mason

Freemasonry, also known as the Masons, is the oldest fraternal organization in the world. Although its origins can be traced back to Medieval times' stonemasons and cathedral builders, Freemasonry remains active in millions of men. Through a series of degrees, the values of Freemasonry are passed from generation to generation, Mason to Mason, in a timeless and tireless effort to make good men better.

I had some free time, and after giving it much thought, I petitioned the Amite City Lodge No. 175 to become a Mason. The Master Masons of the Amite Lodge conducted a background check of mine and conducted interviews with numerous friends of mine. Then came the vote by the lodge members to either accept me as a candidate or decline my membership. Fortunately, I was accepted and notified that my first installment would be the Entered Apprentice Degree.

On March 10, 2005, I was initiated at the Amite City Lodge as an Entered Apprentice (EA), my actual introduction to Masonry. It was a solemn and meaningful ceremony. As an EA, I was entrusted with some of the secrets of the Masonic Order, which were moral and ethical and were expected to be honored according to Masonic law. As an EA, I enjoyed the title of "Brother." My next degree would be the Fellowcraft (FC) Degree.

On April 21, 2005, I passed the rituals of the FC Degree, which refers to skilled members of the craft—literal fellows of the craft. The FC referred to an advanced search for Masonic wisdom, symbolism, and philosophy. This degree would have marked a person's progress from an apprentice to a journeyman, bringing increased responsibility, learning, and work. Upon completing the FC degree, I advanced to the third and final degree, the Master Mason (MM) Degree.

On May 21, 2005, I was elevated to the MM Degree, symbolizing man's maturity in life, age, and increased knowledge and wisdom.

The last lodge ceremonies, the MM degree, completed my initiation ceremonies into the fraternity, and I now enjoy both the rights and responsibilities of membership. As a Master Mason, I had the privilege of visiting lodges worldwide. The picture on the right is of me receiving my Master Mason degree.

On December 14, 2006, after serving as the Senior Deacon, Junior Warden, and Senior Warden, I became the

Worshipful Master of the Amite City Lodge #175. Pictured is Brother Tony Durio (right) presenting me with my Worshipful Master Mason Apron, which I wear whenever I attend a lodge meeting anywhere in the United States.

After receiving my three degrees from my local lodge in Amite, I pursued higher learning by becoming a member of the Scottish Rite in Baton Rouge and working my way up to becoming a 32nd-degree Mason. Being a 32nd-degree Mason meant I had achieved a significant milestone in my journey within the Scottish Rite branch of Freemasonry. To attain my 32nd degree, I had to work my way through from the fourth to the 32nd degree. I had already concluded my first three at my lodge.

A 32nd-degree Mason builds upon the ethical teachings and philosophy offered in the first three degrees of my lodge, and I vow to serve as a person who seeks truth and knowledge, demands freedom of voice, vote, and opinion for all people, and performs my duties to God, country, family, brethren, and myself.

After receiving my 32nd degree, I attended the ritual to become a Knight Templar. This ancient and legitimate Christian order of Knighthood fights today's enemies of society, namely disease and social distress, through charitable efforts and fundraising.

Acacia Shriners

Most people are unaware that to become a member of the Shriners, one must first be a Master Mason. As a Master Mason, I became a member of the Acacia Shrine located in Baton Rouge. As a Shriner, I was involved in and assisted with numerous fundraisers, supporting the Shriners Hospitals for Children.

The Shriners Hospitals for Children is a network of non-profit children's hospitals and other pediatric medical facilities across North America. Children with orthopedic conditions, burns, spinal cord injuries, and cleft lip and palate are eligible for care and receive all services in a family-centered environment, regardless of the patient's ability to pay. Care for children is typically provided until age eighteen, although in some cases, it may be extended to age twenty-one.

The hospital's headquarters is in Tampa, Florida, and it is owned and operated by Shriners International, formerly known as the Ancient Arabic Order of the Nobles of the Mystic Shrine. Shriners are a Freemasonry-related organization whose members are known as Shriners. Patients are not required to be affiliated with the Shriners' Order or involved in Freemasonry.

After being involved with the Shriners for a year, on June 18, 2006, I was installed as an officer of the Acacia Shrine as an "Oriental Guide." Being fourth in the line of succession to become the Potentate of Acacia Shrine within four years.

Shriners are called Nobles, and the Nobles decide in December each year who will be chosen as the Oriental Guide to begin the long move through the Divan to reach the highest post within the Temple, "Potentate."

As stated, when the members of a Shrine Temple elect a Noble to the office of Oriental Guide, they are virtually starting that Noble through the Divan line on the assumption that he

will prove qualified for any merit advancement to the high office of Illustrious Potentate.

The selection of a Nobel for Oriental Guide is quite evident that the nominations should be based upon a thorough and accurate evaluation of the Nobel's character, ability, and interest. A noble can be a fellow, diligent worker, and a loyal Shriner — yet lack the qualifications to make a good potentate. Unless a Noble is fully qualified for the job, it is unfair to him and this Temple to seek the office or permit his fellow Nobles to support and promote his candidacy.

After being appointed the Oriental Guide, I was required to attend the Oriental Guide Leadership Conference held in Tampa, Florida. Linda and I attended in March 2008, and we had a great time during our stay. We met a network of other Oriental Guides from all over the United States. The purpose of the conferences was to provide the knowledge and tools necessary to lead successfully and to prepare for the office of Temple Potentate.

In April 2007, after a year, I was forced to resign from Acacia Shriners and relinquish my position as Oriental Guide. The government notified me that I was transferred from the New Orleans office of Investigations to Headquarters in Washington, DC. With the transfer, I would not be able to fulfill the necessary duties with the Shriners.

My time in the Acacia Shriners was fun. Linda and I attended several Shriners balls and party functions, and the Shriners allowed Linda and me to make many new friends from all over Louisiana, Mississippi, and other states.

While away in Washington, I maintained my membership with Amite City Lodge #175 and attended meetings whenever possible. I also connected with my home lodge and helped with fundraisers or dedicated events whenever possible.

Linda's "MY 50 VET"

On January 27, 2006, I bought Linda a 2002 Chevrolet Corvette for her fiftieth birthday approaching in March. When we lived in Newnan, GA, we owned a 1994 Corvette before we were transferred to the US Virgin Islands. It was advised that we not take the Corvette to the islands, so we sold it because we did not want to put it in storage. I promised Linda I would buy her another Corvette when we returned to the States.

Linda's birthday was March 26th, and although it was a couple of months early, I found a 2002 Corvette available at an import auto dealership in Baton Rouge.

I took Linda there to look at the vehicle. It was in great shape and had low mileage, so we purchased it and drove it home that day.

We celebrated Linda's birthday a little early that year, and when she registered the vehicle, she decided on a specialized license plate that read, "MY 50 VET." This symbolized her fiftieth birthday, but many believed it was Linda's fiftieth Corvette. Many people questioned her about the license plate, and she took the time to explain its meaning.

Right Knee Replacement

Several years earlier, I injured my right knee while working, and I had to have several surgical procedures performed, but nothing corrected my knee problem. The knee was worn out from numerous injuries, but the worker's compensation covered all the treatments and procedures performed.

After the surgeries failed to correct the knee problem, on February 16, 2006, Dr. Thad Broussard from Baton Rouge performed a total right knee replacement at Lady of the Lake Hospital in Baton Rouge. I stayed in the hospital until I was discharged on February 19th, and after extensive therapy, I was able to return to regular work on April 10th.

That knee replacement solved my knee issue, and I was so glad to have it done. The most challenging part was navigating the first six weeks of recovery. When I hit the six-week mark, things seemed to turn around for me, and it started getting easier.

Snake and Massy became Celebrities

On February 21, 2006, Linda received her pet book from Cutest Pets 2005, which featured Snake and Massy's photos.

Linda had previously submitted pictures of the "kids" to the publisher to see if they would make it in the book.

They did not make the cover, but they did make it inside the book. They both became celebrities for a while, with Linda showcasing the book to everyone who stopped by and looked.

The article Linda submitted stated the following; "Our precious "Twins" as we call them, came into our lives after the loss of our dear feline "Sam" whom we loved for eighteen years. We felt that nothing could fill that void, but they stole our hearts and made their own "paw prints in our lives!"

Snake & Massy
submitted by:
Linda Smith

This photo was captured as they snoozed in the sun on a windowsill. I quickly grabbed the hat from an antique doll; you see the rest! With our love of "Victorian," I proudly call this "Snake and Massy…Garden Party."

Linda often dressed these "little Black kids" up for Halloween or any special occasion. They had grown so accustomed to Linda and dressing up that they would sit and allow her to do whatever she wanted with them, even the big 20-pound Snake Man. They did not care because they both knew it made Mommy happy.

Left Kidney Removal

For some time, I had been seeing Dr. Vincent Kidd, a urologist in Hammond, and over the years, he discovered a small spot on my left kidney and began to watch it closely. After watching it for over a year, the spot grew. Dr. Kidd determined, through testing and his opinion, that I had Renal Cell Carcinoma and suggested that the entire kidney be removed to do away with the problem. The spot was located near the artery that fed the kidney, so the only alternative was to remove the entire kidney.

On August 4, 2006, I checked into North Oaks Hospital in Hammond, and Dr. Kidd performed the surgery to remove my kidney. I remained in the hospital until August 7th, when I was allowed to return home. I had to take some time off from work to heal correctly, and then I returned to work on August 28th.

As of today, I have not had any issues with my right kidney, and everything is going well.

I recall the day Dr. Kidd shared the news with me. I was shocked and could not think straight. Dr. Kidd instructed me to walk and then return to talk with him. I stepped outside the office and almost got in my car to leave, thinking that if I could get away from there, this would all go away. It took about fifteen minutes for it to sink in, and I felt things may have changed if I had gone back into the office, but they didn't.

I returned to the doctor's office, and when we talked, he said let's remove the kidney and not worry about it anymore. I agreed with him but wanted to speak with Linda first and explain everything to her. He agreed and said to let him know so we could schedule a surgery date. I went home and told Linda everything, and we both agreed to undergo the surgery. Dr. Kidd removed my left kidney and was able to remove all of the cancer contained inside. Since the surgery, and as of this day, so far, so good.

Detailed Assignment to Washington, DC

On April 1, 2007, I was detailed to the ICE Headquarters and assigned to work in the Asset Forfeiture Unit (AFU). This group at HQ was short-staffed, so agents from the field were detailed to that office to assist with ninety-day assignments.

I reported to Unit Chief David Eoff of the AFU. I was assigned to oversee the twenty-four investigative field offices in the U.S. and assist in seizing assets obtained during criminal investigations.

Linda visited me often in DC, and we did a lot of sightseeing around the area. We visited Arlington Cemetery and watched the guards change. We visited George Washington's home, the State Capitol, the White House, the Washington Monument, the Lincoln Memorial, the Vietnam Wall, the National Cathedral, the National Museum of American History, and all the Smithsonian Museums.

We traveled around the countryside and visited the DC area, taking in all the historical sites. The only time I had off was on weekends, as I was busy all day long on weekdays, starting work at 7:30 a.m. and working until 6 or 7 p.m. every night. The hours in AFU were long and tedious, but I had the weekends off and tried to do as much as possible.

One day, while at work, Unit Chief David Eoff called me into his office and told me that a Section Chief position was becoming available for the office. He asked me if I was interested in the position. As David and I discussed, the position became available. David printed a copy of the announcement and gave it to me for consideration. When he handed it to me, he said, "It's yours if you want it."

I took the announcement and told him I had to think about it and speak with Linda. This would be a significant move for us, so it was only fair to discuss it with Linda before giving my answer to David. I later spoke with Linda about the position and explained that it would give me a substantial raise and upgrade, leading to future advancements. After speaking with Linda, she agreed, so I submitted my application for the position and notified David, who laughed at me and said, "Thanks."

On April 20, 2007, David called me into his office and said, "Congratulations, you have the position." I officially accepted the position for a three-year term with the possibility of two one-year extensions, making it a five-year assignment.

After accepting the position as Section Chief, I returned to New Orleans investigations and informed my squad that I would transfer to the AFU in DC. Everyone in the unit was sad to see me leave, but they understood my reasons, and several agents even tried to follow me to DC.

I received my official transfer orders a few months after I departed for DC, but that was fine because I had a lot to do before then.

Linda and I discussed our options and produced a plan where Linda would stay in Amite while I worked in DC. I knew

In my new position, I would travel frequently, and I learned that I could plan my travels to pass through New Orleans and stay for a few days with Linda before returning to DC. Also, Linda would fly Delta Airlines on a straight flight from New

Orleans to DC, and with my air miles building up, it would not cost her anything to travel to see me.

Working in New Orleans' criminal investigations was enjoyable, and I learned a great deal while supervising some exceptional agents. Still, I eventually had to move on to bigger and better things. Working in DC at AFU provided terrific opportunities for advancement and learning new aspects of the job.

Off to work in DC!

Chapter 15

Asset Forfeiture Unit (AFU)

On August 1, 2007, I reported to the Immigration and Customs Enforcement (ICE) Headquarters in Washington, D.C., as the Section Chief for the Asset Forfeiture Unit (AFU). As Section Chief, I supervised a staff of ICE Senior Special Agents (SSA), Program Managers (PM), Administrative Personnel, and government contractors. I also managed a multi-million-dollar budget from the U.S. Treasury Forfeiture Fund to support ICE's ongoing national forfeitures and investigative programs.

Federal asset forfeiture is a legal tool used by the government to take property connected to criminal activity without compensation; recover property used to compensate victims of the crime; deter, disrupt, and dismantle criminal enterprises; and deprive criminals of the proceeds of their crimes. The program was designed to break the financial backbone of organized criminal syndicates and drug cartels.

The AFU oversaw the asset forfeiture programs in all twenty-six ICE investigative field offices, providing training, support, and guidance on asset forfeiture matters during investigations. I was responsible for the National Systems Control Officers (NSCO), who developed, tested, and

implemented all computer systems related to the Seized Asset Case Management Tracking System used nationwide.

When investigative field offices seize items during their investigations, such as houses, cars, assorted property, animals (including horses or cattle), and money, we at AFU assume total control and management of those assets. Once all the items are collected, we calculate their monetary value and then distribute the proceeds among all the participating agencies involved in the case.

One of the most essential functions I had as Section Chief was to ensure that seizures were both fiscally responsible and legally sound, able to withstand public and legal scrutiny. We had to ensure that the investigative field offices gathered evidence during the investigation and planned for the legal and logistical aspects of seizures and forfeitures.

That office must also consider the economic impact of each seizure, including the cost of management, storage, depreciation, and disposal of the seized property. An example would be seizing a vehicle worth more than its value. In this case, seizing the vehicle would not be feasible because it would incur a cost to the government.

Field Office Inspections

The AFU also conducted field office inspections as part of the asset seizure and forfeiture investigations. The inspections were crucial for identifying and seizing assets linked to criminal activities and ensuring that the field offices adhered to federal laws and ICE regulations.

As the Section Chief for the AFU, I conduct field office inspections for the twenty-six field offices, along with their suboffices, across the United States, Hawaii, Guam, Puerto Rico, and the U.S. Virgin Islands. The field inspection included reviewing the seized property rooms, where evidence was stored, and other seized items. We would review how the evidence and seized property were collected and processed before storing them. Seized property rooms had to be a specific size and equipped with the necessary locks, sensors, and video surveillance equipment for security and safety. Property housed in these rooms had to be accurately logged and maintained per ICE policy and procedures. Depending on the office size and the amount of seized property being stored, inspections took one day or less; however, some larger offices required up to three days or more.

Federal Air Marshal (FAM)

Before September 11, 2001, while traveling with our service weapons on official government duty, all we had to do was check in at the airline's counter, provide our credentials, and fill out the necessary paperwork to fly armed. After checking in with the airline, we would walk around the TSA security checkpoint and check in with the local police agency stationed at the airport security counter. We signed the logbook with the officer and boarded our flight at our gate. We arrived at the entrance and provided the airline with a copy of our paperwork, declaring that we were armed as law enforcement officers (LEOs).

Flying as a LEO often meant I was in first class or a seat on an aisle or exit aisle. In the first class, we ate well, but of course, we could not have alcohol, and we had to stay awake/alert for the entire flight.

Meridian at Braddock Station

I lived in a high-rise apartment complex called Meridian at Braddock Station, situated on the Braddock Station Metrorail train route.

Metrorail was a safe and reliable transit service for me traveling throughout Washington, D.C. The DC Metrorail system had 98 stations in Virginia, Maryland, and the District of Columbia.

The Metrorail system had six color-coded rail lines: Red, Orange, Silver, Blue, Yellow, and Green. The system's layout allowed travel between two or more stations without a single transfer.

Before moving to D.C., I purchased a 2006 Chevy HHR from Hoods in Amite. A friend of mine, Ken Miller, sold me the vehicle because I planned to drive it from my apartment to work daily and use it on weekends. Linda and I drove it to Alexandria and kept it there for me to drive.

Driving to work each day was murder because of the high volume of traffic and all the stop-and-go vehicles. It would take me an hour to get to work and park, even though the office was only a few miles from my apartment. One day, sitting in traffic, I noticed the Metrorail passing me nonstop. It gave me a thought: why not try the Metrorail one day for work and see how that works out? Well, I did. Riding the Metrorail was the fastest way to get to work. So, I began using the Metrorail daily, even on weekends when I would go downtown. I could take the train from my apartment and get off at a station near my destination. It was just that easy!

After discovering my new mode of transportation, I found that

I was not using the HHR and was paying to park it at my apartment complex. Eventually, I brought the HHR back to Amite, and Linda started using it. As it turned out, the HHR became Linda's favorite vehicle, and she drives it everywhere.

Even today, she declares the HHR her favorite vehicle. The HHR runs excellent, and we have never had a problem since we purchased it. It could use a paint job, and there are a few dents, but it's still Linda's favorite.

Every day, I would walk out of my apartment building and go to the Braddock Station Metrorail to catch the work train. I rode the train daily, and the government paid for my Metrorail expenses. When I first moved into the building, I leased a studio apartment on the 22nd floor. I chose the studio because there was more than enough room for me, and even when Linda came to visit, we had plenty of room for the two of us.

After about a year of living in the studio apartment, a larger studio apartment, including a sunroom, became available on the ground floor of the building. So, I moved into that apartment and enjoyed the extra living area with the sunroom.

It took me time to adapt to living in an apartment and that lifestyle. The good news was that the walls were thick, and the noise from the neighbors was minimal.

The building had a large exercise room for tenants to use, and I had a great opportunity to exercise. Besides the gym, it had a large outdoor swimming pool next to it. I used the exercise room frequently because it helped me relax and relieve stress from daily work.

On weekends, I would visit the Smithsonian museums downtown. There were days I would spend the entire day inside one museum. The Smithsonian is a group of museums created by the U.S. government and founded on August 10, 1846. It operates as a trust and is not formally part of any of the three branches of the federal government. The institution was named after its founding donor, British scientist James Smithson.

The Smithsonian includes the National Museum of Natural History, the National Museum of American History, the National Air and Space Museum, the National Museum of African Art, the National Postal Museum, the National Museum of the American Indian, the National Museum of

African American History and Culture, and the National Museum of the American Latino, and the Smithsonian American Women's History Museum.

On some weekends, I would pick out one museum and spend the entire day observing everything on display. I would not leave until I had seen every item. I would also have lunch at the museum and enjoy the day, taking in all the sights.

I often walked over to the White House or the Washington Monument and sat on a bench to watch people. People from all over the world were walking around in the Mall area and in front of the Capitol Building, and you could see anything and everything, just people-watching.

The National Mall is a landscaped park near downtown that borders several Smithsonian museums, art galleries, cultural institutions, and various memorials, sculptures, and statues. The National Park Service of the United States Department of the Interior oversees it as part of the National Mall and Memorial Parks unit of the National Park System. The core area of the National Mall, extending between the U.S. Capitol grounds and the Washington Monument, is lined by several museums and federal office buildings.

There were Sundays when I would walk over to the Supreme Court Building and sit on a park bench, observing the uniqueness of the buildings. I often told myself how lucky I was to see all the historical buildings in D.C., as there was so much to see and take in while walking around the mall. There are numerous buildings and statues to visit, including the Lincoln Memorial, the World War II Memorial, the Vietnam Veterans Memorial, the National Air and Space Museum, the National Cathedral, and many more.

When Linda came to visit me, we took numerous tours. We went everywhere. We visited Georgetown University and George Washington's home in Alexandria, VA.

We made numerous trips to see the White House (left) and other notable monuments and government buildings downtown. On weekends, there was always something to do and see, such as watching protesters march around protesting something. " There could also be a parade for any reason, and

street entertainers were always performing on every corner, which was fun to watch.

Another fun fact about walking around downtown was the assorted restaurants. They were everywhere, and we often stood around trying to decide where to eat. It was a hard decision, for sure. I recall visiting the mall's grassy area in the fall and watching the rugby games. One day, after a freezing rain, I watched those guys go out there and play in that cold, wet mud. I stood on the sidelines and could hear them hitting each other with no protective pads or helmets, and they were grown men out there playing, not children. Watching the games played in the mud was fun; however, the cloudy conditions and light wind on a fall day made me too cold to stay long. I admit that I could never stay and watch the entire game. It was too brutal for me!

Linda and I visited and toured the Washington Monument to view the entire city from its top point. The views were outstanding; one window offered a direct view of the White House, another faced the Lincoln Memorial, and a third looked toward the Capitol. The other view was toward the Jefferson Memorial and the Washington Reagan Airport. We took many pictures and videos from the top of the monument, and whenever someone visited us, we tried to take them up for the view.

Special Investigations Unit (SIU)

One day in late August 2008, while I was working in AFU, I was contacted by William Metzger, Chief of the Special Investigations Unit (SIU) for The Office of Professional Responsibility (OPR), Washington, D.C. Chief Metzger said they were looking to fill a position within SIU, and after reviewing my background, he thought I would be a good fit. Chief Metzger stated that the Associate Director of Investigations, who was over at AFU and several other divisions at HQ, referred my name to him. After receiving the recommendation, he conducted a review and now wanted to know if I would be interested in conducting investigations at OPR SIU in DC.

OPR is the internal affairs division for DHS/ICE employees. SIU investigated allegations against Senior management officials at the GS-14 or Executive Services (ES) level.

After speaking with Chief Metzger, I discussed it with Chief Oaff and numerous others, and everyone recommended that I take the position. Although Chief Oaff did not want to lose me, he gave me his blessings. After significant consideration and discussion with Linda, I accepted the position and returned to what I love doing: investigations. After receiving my official transfer orders, I packed my belongings at AFU and moved to SIU in Arlington, VA.

My coworkers and staff at AFU gave me a going-away party, complete with a cake, and presented me with a plaque in recognition of my dedicated service to AFU. I enjoyed AFU and supervising all those employees, but I am a criminal investigator and love conducting case interviews. So, getting out of the management role and back into the investigator position was a thrill. During my tenure at AFU, I gained extensive experience managing millions of dollars in funds and supervising a team of employees. It was added to my resume, and I was able to maintain my grade as a GS-14 with my 25% law enforcement availability pay.

Snowstorm 2008

While I waited for my official transfer papers, we experienced a terrific snowstorm or blizzard in DC. I took many pictures and videos of the storm because I had never experienced such weather. I experienced two storms back-to-back while living in DC.

During the first storm, I was sitting in my apartment looking out the sunroom window when I saw someone walking on the sidewalk through the snow and blizzard. At the time, at least three feet of snow was on the ground, and more fell fast. I looked away for a second, and when I looked back, the person had disappeared. I looked around and wondered where that person had gone so quickly. Then, I saw a place where the snow was moving on the ground as if someone were buried underneath. The snow on the ground in that area moved again; by then, I could tell that the person had fallen and was covered in the snow. I noticed the person struggling to stand up because they kept slipping and falling. The person

stopped moving at one point while I watched through my window.

Out of concern, I grabbed my shoes and a coat and ran outside. I crossed the building parking lot and ran across the street where I thought the individual was lying. There was so much snow that I could not tell where the curb or street began. I stepped slowly and carefully so I would not get hurt. I finally reached the spot where I remembered the person lying and had to dig through the snow. I eventually found the person lying on their belly, so I helped them to stand up. That is when I noticed it was an elderly female wrapped up in clothes and a large blanket. When I stood her up, the wind blew so hard that I couldn't hear or understand what she was trying to tell me. It was snowing so hard that it was difficult to see around you. I knew there was a McDonald's on the corner, so I was able to help her get to the restaurant. We got inside, and I sat her in a booth where she thanked me. After catching her breath, she told me she was trying to walk to McDonald's to get coffee.

She said she slipped and fell and couldn't get herself off the ground.

I went to the counter and ordered her coffee, but she could not find her purse and started crying. She said that she must have dropped it when she fell. I had no money because I grabbed my shoes and a coat when I left my apartment. The young man working the counter said, "Forget it," and gave her the coffee. I sat with the lady for a while, ensuring she was all right. She said she would stay there and call her son to pick her up. At the time, her phone was inside her purse, but we had planned for her to use it at the restaurant. After getting her situated, I decided to start that walk back to my apartment.

When I left the woman and walked back toward my apartment, I stopped where the woman was lying on the ground. I searched the area, and luckily, I found the woman's small purse on the ground. I picked it up and returned to McDonald's to bring it to her. It took me a while to return because the storm was terrible, with strong winds and heavy snow blowing around. When I returned to her, she was so grateful and offered me a few dollars to find the purse, but I declined. She offered to buy me a meal, but I thanked her and declined, then sat and talked with her for a few more minutes before leaving.

I left McDonald's and started my way back to my apartment.

Eventually, when I made it back, I couldn't help but think what could have happened if I hadn't seen the woman fall. No one was around the area, and if I hadn't seen where she fell, she would have lain there in the snow and died. I like to think that I was used by the Lord that day to help the woman stay safe.

Working at AFU was a terrific learning experience. It taught me much about asset sharing with other agencies and supervising designated programs from the headquarters level. I met many people and made many friends. After receiving my official transfer orders, I reported to SIU to begin my next chapter.

Chapter 16

Special Investigation Unit (SIU)

Office of Professional Responsibility (OPR)

On October 12, 2008, I was officially assigned to the SIU at Immigration and Customs Enforcement (ICE), Office of Professional Responsibility (OPR), Arlington, VA.

OPR is the internal affairs division of the Department of Homeland Security (DHS). Special Agents (Criminal Investigators) coordinate and conduct highly complex, challenging, and sensitive criminal, civil, and administrative investigations involving alleged misconduct, criminal activity, and/or corruption by Department of Homeland Security (DHS) employees and related entities.

OPR consists of employees from both the government and private sectors. Its diverse team of Special Agents conducts thorough, unbiased, and professional investigations to support its overall mission of safeguarding and promoting the integrity and security of the DHS workforce. OPR meets this mission by ensuring accountability and building strong partnerships guided by the principles of professionalism, responsibility, and integrity.

Typical Assignments handled by OPR include gathering and analyzing vital information, facts, evidence, an intelligence from various sources, such as law enforcement and government-specific databases, crime scene and use-of-force incidents, and thorough interviews with subject and witness employees. Our OPR cases involved investigating incidents involving lethal and non-lethal force, from response to incident processing and preparing appropriate investigative reports.

We utilized all of the agency's authorities and capabilities, enabling us to support investigations into criminal corruption, employee misconduct, counterterrorism, and counterintelligence that directly impacted national security and agency integrity. We created reports of investigations and testified in court or other proceedings regarding our investigative findings.

We also conducted investigations of major interregional dimensions with national or international implications. This included investigating individuals, businesses, employees, and criminal organizations that represent a significant threat to the United States' national security through corruption or attempted corruption, including foreign intelligence organizations and terrorist groups seeking to compromise federal personnel.

Now, SIU is an OPR HQ-based unit located in Arlington, VA., and we investigate allegations involving DHS senior executives and other sensitive, high-profile investigative matters. The SIU investigations often involve critical incidents and significant cases likely to generate media, congressional, or departmental interest, both domestically and internationally.

Mexico City

On March 23, 2009, I was assigned an SIU case and had to travel to Mexico City to interview the American Embassy employees. I interviewed seven individuals regarding an allegation that originated in D.C., but all the individuals I interviewed were either currently stationed at the embassy or had been there on business. It was great to catch up with them all while I was there.

While conducting my interviews at the embassy, the then-Secretary of State Hillary Clinton was visiting. One afternoon, one of the Assistant Ambassadors asked me if I would meet and greet Clinton cordially in the receiving line with other employees. I had no desire to meet her, but since I was asked to go, I figured I would be polite and go to get in line.

After finishing one of my interviews that afternoon, I went to the receiving line with the other employees to meet Clinton. Another agent was assigned to assist me with my interviews, and he accompanied me, but neither of us wanted to be there. We were busy conducting interviews and wanted to finish so we could go home. While standing in line, we eventually worked our way up close to meeting Clinton, and I noticed an open door to my right, and no one was standing around that area. So, I veered off to the right and went straight for the open door. When I finished and stopped to figure out where I was going next, the other agent ran into me from behind because he was following me with the same idea. We then walked away and made our way back to conduct our interviews.

Visiting the White House and the Capitol

On September 15, 2009, Linda and I visited the White House. We walked, toured, and observed the building inside and out, but didn't go upstairs to the living quarters. Walking through the facility and entering all the rooms downstairs was pretty exciting. We went into the public rooms in the East Wing and the Residence, which include the Vermeil Room, the Library, the China Room, the Blue Room, the Red Room, the Green Room, the State Dining Room, and a view of the White House

Kennedy Garden. A Secret Service agent was stationed along the tour route and was available to answer questions about each room's history, art, furnishings, current uses, and other aspects. It was a lot of fun!

On September 18, 2009, we visited the U.S. Capitol building and completed a tour. After our tour, we met and befriended one of the Capitol Police Officers, who offered to take us around the Capitol building and into rooms and locations where the general public was not usually allowed entry. The officer also took us out onto the balcony of the Capitol building, where we stood and took plenty of pictures. We were taken to a room that housed a large bathtub used by President William Howard Taft because of his size. It was a very extensive tour, and I later sent him a thank-you note expressing how much we had enjoyed his tour.

National Archives Building

I took Linda to the National Archives building one day, and we toured the entire building. The National Archives & Records Administration Building is north of the National Mall. The Administration preserves, protects, and shares the historical federal records of the United States.

I researched that the National Archives is home to billions of records, including the three most important documents in

American history: the Declaration of Independence, the U.S. Constitution, and the Bill of Rights. We observed these in the Rotunda for the Charters of Freedom at the National Archives Building. That was a fun day, and seeing those documents you read about in school and watching movies regarding the signing of the Constitution was incredible. I'm so glad we had the opportunity to go there.

Transfer to Houston

On March 26, 2010, I received a phone call from Sean Quick, the Deputy Director (DD) for OPR, asking if I wanted

to transfer to Houston with the OPR Management Inspection Unit (MIU). DD Quick and I had become good friends, and he knew I wanted to get back closer to Louisiana. He stated that OPR aimed to establish a new MIU office in Houston to increase the number of offices nationwide. He told me I would set up the office and prepare for the arrival of other employees. I accepted the opportunity on the spot, but it meant I would have to leave investigations and work with the MIU. OPR Investigations already had a large office established in Houston, and they had several unused offices in their building that MIU could use to set up shop.

After receiving my transfer notice, I coordinated with the moving company to arrange packing and moving. On May 4,

2010, the moving packers came to my apartment and packed my belongings for shipment. I remember that day well because I was excited to move back closer to Louisiana and the South. Linda also supervised the packing efforts and kept everyone in line.

At the office, the SIU agents gave me a going-away party on May 7th, where we had plenty of food and a large cake. They also presented me with a large plaque featuring a photo of downtown D.C., embedded with an OPR SIU challenge coin, and a small plaque bearing my name, expressing their gratitude for the service I provided to SIU.

On May 17th, the moving van arrived and loaded my belongings from the apartment, which were then shipped to Houston. We are Houston bound!!

Chapter 17

OPR Management Inspections Unit (MIU)

On May 17, 2010, after the movers picked up my belongings from my D.C. apartment, Linda and I flew to New Orleans. Chuck and Mary Ellen Brister met us at the airport to drive us to Amite. We spent the day together, taking it easy so we could prepare for our trip to Houston.

On May 19th, we traveled to Baytown, Texas, and checked into the Best Western Baytown hotel. We stayed there while searching for an apartment in the Baytown area. We chose Baytown because it was on the southeast side of Houston, making it easier for us to travel back and forth to Amite. We examined many apartment complexes but couldn't find one that met our needs.

On May 20th, we went out searching again, and this time, we found our apartment at Villas at Rolling brook, located at 3717 Emmet Hutto Blvd., Baytown. It seemed like a nice, quiet location, but it was off the primary areas of Baytown. It was also close to grocery shopping and restaurants, and driving to my new office was easy. After signing the lease, we had to wait for the delivery of our furniture from DC.

On May 27th, our furniture finally arrived at our new apartment. After the movers had unloaded our belongings, we began to settle in. It took some time to get used to living there. It was a brand-new apartment, and we were the first to move in. It had hardwood floors, one bedroom, one bath, and a large living room.

Linda drove back and forth from Baytown to Amite with Snake and Massy in tow. She would come to stay for a while in Baytown and then return to Amite to check on our home there. I would drive to Amite on long weekends and spend time away from work. Linda and I took turns traveling back and forth, staying at both locations. I also had much leeway at work to travel and work. I would often fly around the country and frequently fly into New Orleans on my way back to Houston. I would then ride with Linda over to Baytown because this gave us time to spend with each other,

My First Day at Work

On May 28th, I reported to work as a Senior Special Agent at MIU for my first day. I met with the Resident Agent in Charge (RAC) for OPR investigations, who showed me around the office, including the three offices designated for me to set up the MIU offices.

Several days after I arrived, two other special agents assigned to work at MIU assisted me in setting up the new office. OPR headquarters had previously sent numerous boxes containing office supplies, file cabinets, desks, and assorted government forms for MIU use. Eventually, our main computers and programs arrived, and we began setting up our new MIU office.

After several weeks of sorting, arranging, and organizing the office, we were ready to assume our official duties. At this point, HQ started sending us our work assignments. We were officially up and running as an MIU office.

The MIU Duties

MIU agents inspected ICE directorates, programs, and field offices to verify and ensure compliance with established federal, departmental, agency, or program-specific policies and procedures. Our MIU inspections highlight to ICE leadership any areas that need attention, resources, or improvement in the office we inspected.

When we conducted our MIU inspections, we included

financial audits of agency Certified Undercover Operations to ensure that the undercover financial activities were adequately accounted for in accordance with law and agency policy.

We conducted on-site field office inspections of domestic and international ICE field offices and ICE Headquarters Units. The inspection process involved a comprehensive review of operational and administrative practices to provide ICE senior managers with an independent assessment of the office's internal controls, effectiveness, and efficiency.

During my brief tenure at MIU, from May 28, 2010, to February 1, 2011, I made numerous trips around the country to perform inspections of ICE field offices. Those offices included Atlanta, Boston, Buffalo, Chicago, Cleveland, Denver, El Paso, Guam, Hawaii, Las Vegas, Long Beach, CA, Nogales, San Antonio, Seattle, Tampa, and many more.

The inspection process typically took three to five days, and my position was to interview employees working in those offices to determine their knowledge of policies and procedures. These interviews were conducted more as informal talks than formal interviews, allowing me to determine if the office required additional training or resources.

Linda and I did a lot of sightseeing around Houston and the surrounding area. We frequented many restaurants in Baytown and Houston, and we even had a special Mexican restaurant in Baytown that we would visit every weekend.

On February 2, 2011, I received a phone call late that afternoon from ICE OPR Deputy Director Sean Quick, who asked if I wanted to return to investigations and work at the OPR New Orleans field office. I told him I could be there that night and ready to go the next day, but he laughed at me and told me to clear out my case reports for the MIU inspections we were conducting, and he would be back in touch with me soon.

I enjoyed living in Baytown and working in Houston, specifically at MIU. I would have been comfortable working in the Houston office if the New Orleans position hadn't come. I couldn't pass up the opportunity to return to Amite and live in my home again. Additionally, the New Orleans OPR office has reinstated me to conduct investigations, where I wanted to be. The ten months we spent there were enjoyable, and we would do it all over again.

I received my official transfer orders to OPR New Orleans several days later. I immediately started packing for New Orleans. I planned to arrive by early March and live in my Amite home.

Headed to OPR investigations in New Orleans.

CHAPTER 18

OPR Investigations New Orleans, LA

I was thrilled when OPR Assistant Director Sean Quick called me in Houston about transferring to the New Orleans OPR office. I expected the transfer to take months, but I received my orders within weeks. I planned to arrive in New Orleans by early March 2011, where I would live in Amite and commute daily.

The OPR New Orleans (OPRNO) Investigations office was located on the 22nd floor of the Entergy Building, at the intersection of Loyola and Poydras Streets in downtown New Orleans. My office had a great view of the Superdome and downtown, allowing me to see Mardi Gras parades and immigration protests below.

My OPR Duties

The OPRNO cases I was assigned were similar to those I worked on with the SIU. However, I had a five-state area of responsibility in New Orleans, investigating allegations related to all DHS/ICE employees and other criminal accusations. These states included Louisiana, Mississippi, Arkansas, Tennessee, and Alabama, encompassing thirty-five ICE offices. Additionally, numerous ICE detention facilities were located within these states, housing several thousand detainees awaiting deportation or immigration hearings.

At OPRNO, we collaborated with internal and external programs and offices to ensure that misconduct allegations against employees were addressed appropriately, fairly, and expeditiously. We also reviewed all the critical incidents, such as employee-involved shootings, that occurred within the ICE offices in our area.

Our reviews documented the events that transpired during critical incidents, and when needed, reviews were presented to the ICE Firearms and Use of Force Incident Review Committee for action.

OPRNO examined issues that could lead to criminal prosecution or significant administrative misconduct, which an ICE manager would address.

We managed the Prison Rape Elimination Act (PREA) program, coordinating with OPR offices and other investigative entities to address sexual assault allegations involving ICE detainees.

The New Orleans OPR office comprises three special agents, a supervisory special agent, and an investigative assistant.

Before my report day, Linda and I visited my office to familiarize ourselves with the environment and meet the team. All of my shipped belongings were inside the office. I planned for Linda to return soon to assist with moving in and setting up the office.

First Day at Work

I started work on March 14, 2011, and it took me several days to become familiar with the office's layout and procedures. I quickly set up my computer to access the necessary applications, which took about a week to function fully.

One Saturday morning, Linda and I went to my office and unboxed all my belongings. Linda handled the interior decorating, making the office appear formal, official, and homely. She hung pictures, moved furniture, and placed an American flag on the wall. Linda performed her tasks effectively.

With Linda being my interior designer, the agents in the office were jealous because their offices didn't look as professional as mine. The other agents would come around in the afternoons and stop by my door to stare into my office, admiring what Linda had done.

I know they picked up a few ideas because their offices made some changes for the better.

When I arrived at OPRNO, the Resident Agent in Charge (RAC) position for New Orleans was vacant, and ICE HQ sought to fill the role promptly.

The RAC is responsible for supervising the office's daily operations and monitoring all the OPR cases within the jurisdiction. It ultimately took two years after my arrival to fill the position.

In the interim, the two other agents and I alternated as the acting RAC, each serving three-month rotations. This arrangement allowed us to manage our cases and effectively fulfill office responsibilities as needed.

When the position was finally filled, it relieved a lot of pressure. We could focus on our cases and let the RAC handle everyday operations.

I can't discuss every case I worked on while assigned to OPRNO, but I would like to highlight a couple that particularly interested me. I would estimate that I completed several hundred investigations at New Orleans OPR.

Receiving the Assistant Director's Award

On April 2, 2014, I received the Assistant Director's "2013 Excellence in Investigation Award" from the U.S. Department of Homeland Security for my work on the DO prostitution cases. The ceremony occurred at the DHS office in New Orleans, where Assistant Director Tim Moynihan and Special Agent in Charge David D'Amato presented the award.

The Assistant Director's Award recognizes the significant contributions of an employee who has advanced the mission of the Department of Homeland Security, Homeland Security Investigations, during the year.

During the presentation, Assistant Director Moynihan said I had performed above and beyond the call of duty by conducting significant and diverse high-profile investigations that I had pursued thoroughly, tirelessly, and professionally. AD Moynihan said, "I was a determined agent with tremendous interview skills, and I encompassed all the qualities of what a Special Agent should be."

AD Moynihan mentioned I was also a Certified Forensic Interviewer for the Department of Homeland Security. I traveled extensively throughout the United States, conducting interviews about suspected criminal activity.

Conducting criminal or administrative investigations takes time to prepare, either for the U.S. Attorney in criminal cases or for the District Director of OPR in administrative cases.

Returning $9,800

On October 30, 2020, I was assigned to work on a criminal case in Fort Smith, Arkansas. While traveling through a small town just outside McGehee, Arkansas, my partner and I stopped at an Amish grocery store to use the restroom and get a sandwich. They made great sandwiches, and we always stopped by this place whenever we passed through on our way to Fort Smith. I went to the restroom and found a wallet lying on the floor. I picked it up and discovered it contained $9,800 in $100 bills. I then examined the wallet to see if it contained any identification of the possible owner. I found nothing but a check stub from a high school in Monticello, Arkansas. No name or other form of identification was on the stub or wallet. On the outside of the wallet was the Mississippi State Bulldogs football team logo.

I held on to the wallet and asked everyone in the store if they had lost one, but no one answered. Upon leaving the store, I decided to call the school in Monticello to see if anyone had lost a wallet or to obtain some information about the potential owner. I spoke with a security guard at the school, and after talking with him for a while, he informed me that a now-retired principal would often leave his wallet around. However, he has since retired, and the security guard had no clue where to find him. I happened to ask the guard if he knew what the ex-principal's wallet looked like, and he said he didn't remember the color, but he did recall that there was a team logo on the outside. After telling me this, I advised him that I had a wallet with a team logo on the outside that contained cash inside. The guard went to the school office and obtained the ex-principal's last known phone number and address.

After obtaining the information from the guard, we continued our journey to Fort Smith. I called the number I received and left a message stating that I had found a wallet at the Amish store and that he should call me back if he had lost one. Several hours later, this man called me, excited and talking so fast that

I could barely understand him. He advised me that he had lost his wallet somewhere, but it was a brown wallet with the Mississippi Bulldog logo.

He then stated that he had $9,800 inside, in $100 bills. I never told anyone how much money was in the wallet or described the color. This gentleman stated that he was a retired school principal from Monticello High School, and he had just withdrawn the money from the bank to purchase musical instruments for his church band, intending to surprise them with the gift. He stated that when he arrived at the musical instrument store, he realized he had left his wallet at home, so he searched his car and called his wife to help him locate it. Then he received a call from me saying I had found a wallet.

After he had identified the wallet, money, and logo, I advised him that I was in Fort Smith and would be back in that

area in a couple of days. We made arrangements to meet at the Amish store, and on November 1st, I gave the man his money, and he and his wife cried in appreciation. He offered me a reward during our meeting, which I graciously declined. The store where I found his wallet is in the photo's background.

God used me that day to find and return that wallet to its owner. We almost didn't stop that day because we were in a hurry, but I decided to stop anyway. I am so glad I did. I never thought of keeping the money and saying nothing for a minute because I knew God wanted me to find it and return it to its owner.

Linda's New Corvette

When we left Newnan, GA, for the Virgin Islands, we sold a 2002 Corvette before leaving, as we did not want to take it to the islands. I promised Linda we would get a new Corvette when we returned to the States. In early 2012, now that we were living back in Amite, it was time to purchase the new Corvette I had promised Linda. I contacted my good friend, Ken Miller, who sold cars for Hood's Chevrolet in Amite. Ken had sold me all my previous vehicles, and he and I became good friends. When I contacted Ken, I specified the type of Corvette I was looking for, namely a 2012 Grand Sport, and described the color and all the features I wanted in the vehicle. After speaking with him, I figured it would be a while before he got back to me, so I forgot about our conversation.

Early the next morning, I was at work in New Orleans when Linda called, saying a new Corvette was sitting in our driveway.

She said Ken told her to drive it for a few days, and if we wanted to keep it, we could do the paperwork later. When I got home that afternoon, we drove around and decided to keep it.

I called Ken the next day and told him we wanted it. Several days later, we went to Hoods and signed the papers.

Our friend Ken has since passed away. He was a good man to do business with and was never pushy or tried to convince you to buy anything. He was several years older than we were, and he and Linda were extremely fond of each other. Every time I was looking for a new vehicle, Ken was the first person I went to. He would find it if he had the car I wanted on his lot.

Our Amtrak Vacation

One day at work, I thought it was time to take a vacation. Linda had never ridden an Amtrak train, so she and I talked about it, and we decided to take a train trip around the western half of the country. I then started researching different trips and ways to travel, but it got easier when I contacted Amtrak and had them make my arrangements for us. Not long after speaking with Amtrak, the trip was booked, and the travel date was set.

On June 7, 2014, Linda and I took our Amtrak vacation around the western United States. We began our trip by departing from New Orleans and traveling to Chicago, Minneapolis, and Seattle. We spent a day in Seattle, touring the city and taking a tour of the Space Needle. We also had a friend living in Seattle who was a traveling nurse and had moved to the Virgin Islands when we were there.

We boarded the train the next day and left Seattle, heading

southward to Los Angeles. We got off the train and spent an extra day touring the city. We traveled all over Los Angeles with a tour group and visited numerous historical sites, including the Hollywood Sign on the hillside.

The next morning, we left Los Angeles and traveled East along the southern border, passing through the small town of Marfa, TX., my first duty station on the Border Patrol. We continued along the southern border while eventually returning to New Orleans.

It was a fun trip for us riding on the train. We traveled in a sleeper car with a huge picture window for sightseeing. Two beds were pulled down for sleeping at night, and we ate most of our meals in the dining car. We sometimes had dinner in our sleeper car, which was more private, and showered at night before converting it into our sleeping quarters.

The train made numerous stops along the West Coast route, and at each stop, we could step off and stretch our legs or, at times, even tour the area in small towns. Sometimes, the stops were just for a few minutes or even lasted fifteen minutes or more, but it was always time to step off and take a walk.

Taking a vacation for a while was beneficial because we were remarkably busy at work, and taking a little time off was a welcome respite. We returned to New Orleans on June 15th, and I resumed my work routine.

Vacation to Branson, MO

On November 6, 2015, Linda and I traveled to Branson to escape for a few days. We owned a 29-foot travel trailer and pulled it to Branson during this time. We stayed at one of the nearby trailer parks.

We obtained show tickets, went sightseeing, and toured the Titanic Museum. The museum provided detailed information about the Titanic's history. Upon entering, we received a card with the name of an individual who was either a survivor or a victim of the actual ship. By the end of the tour, we learned the person's fate on our cards. The museum in Branson offered insight into the events of the Titanic's sinking while honoring those who lost their lives. We plan to return and visit the Titanic Museum again. We went on a dinner cruise on the Showboat Branson Belle. The paddlewheel boat was completely modeled after the old ships of the 1800s. This cruise was a fantastic way for us to get out and experience the views of Table Rock Lake.

The ship was immaculate and comfortable, and we had a great time. The vessel was 112 feet tall and 278 feet long, with its two twin paddle wheels measuring 16 feet in diameter. They stated that the vessel can accommodate up to 700 passengers and reach speeds of up to 11 knots. During our dinner, we enjoyed live entertainment along with delicious food.

The cruise dock was located at White River Landing Table Rock Lake, which offered numerous shops for visitors. Table Rock Lake is 43,100 acres with 745 miles of shoreline. The artificial lake was created by Table Rock Dam, which the White River feeds.

Alabama Randy Owens Ranch

On June 25, 2016, Linda and I had the opportunity to visit the ranch in Ft. Payne, AL, belonging to Randy Owens, a member of the country band Alabama. Randy was a band member, and we spent the day on his ranch.

Owens hosted a large cookout featuring hamburgers and hot dogs for his fan club, to which Linda was a member. We had a good barbecue, and after the cookout, Owens put on a small concert in a barn. He had a few other musical guests perform before him, and they were all very good. We sat in bleachers in the barn with all the other fan club members, and it was a fun time. We were fairly close to the bands and took plenty of pictures.

Conclusion

Regarding my criminal and administrative cases in OPRNO, I conducted thorough investigations and adhered to principles of fairness. All individuals involved were treated honestly and with respect, and many acknowledged to my superiors the respectful treatment they received.

I ensured everyone involved was treated fairly and unbiasedly in OPR internal affairs investigations. The investigation should be conducted impartially.

When investigating allegations against an ICE employee, acknowledging dignity is the first step in having empathy. Empathy is the capacity to understand another person by imagining yourself in their situation. It enables you to feel their agony and sincerely offer help and support. In many cases, I worked on involving employees; that is precisely what I felt. I put myself in their situation to understand what they were going through. I worked closely with many coworkers and ICE employees, sharing personal details about my life with them. However, although I was unfamiliar with the details of their home, family situation, or core values, I still showed empathy. I treated them as if I understood their difficulties.

In every OPR case I investigated, I treated everyone as a human being, which increased my safety, reduced my stress, enhanced my work satisfaction, improved my job performance, and strengthened my relationships with the people I encountered. When I treated people with dignity, I found that they were more likely to cooperate with my requests, remain calm during interviews, and treat me well in return.

I admit that the majority turned out as they should have, but some took unexpected turns. I could never tire of discussing my cases, the people involved, and my experiences investigating them. Some of the cases I had caused me to travel to many ICE offices throughout the United States, including numerous U.S. embassies.

I spent 10 years, 9 months, and 16 days working in the OPR NO office. I saw agents come and go, and many changes took place there. Regarding the cases I was assigned, I could spend days discussing each and its outcome.

In internal affairs, I knew that poorly conducted investigations can lead to serious consequences. Employee investigations are essential for resolving workplace issues, but it's important to be compassionate toward employees involved in the process. Focusing on the human aspect can improve the quality of your investigation. It is worth noting that a poorly run investigation can harm more than one person.

Treating people with dignity means treating them as you want to be treated. Everyone has the right to lead a dignified life and fulfill their potential.

I worked in OPR NO from March 14, 2011, until I retired on December 31, 2022. Before I retired, I was the oldest Senior Special Agent working for the federal government as a GS-14, Step 10, with an additional 25% Administratively Uncontrollable Overtime (AUO).

Retirement! Here it is. I never thought I would see the day. Well, it's time for me to go and explore my new adventure: retirement.

Chapter 19

Retirement

From my start at the Amite Police Department to my retirement with the Department of Homeland Security, Immigration and Customs Enforcement, spanning forty-six years, I have met many people and made more friends than I can imagine. But work had to end sometime.

Throughout all the years I worked, I never thought about retiring because I always figured I wouldn't live long enough to reach that stage. I consistently maintained excellent life insurance throughout my tenure because I wanted Linda to be cared for in my absence. Given that most of my relatives rarely lived past sixty, I anticipated a similar fate. Rather than planning for retirement, I focused on securing a reliable life insurance policy. After many years of working for the government, I didn't intend to retire and draw my benefits.

Consequently, I never made any retirement plans.

Then, in March and April 2022, a light went off in my head. I thought, Donnie, it was time for you to go. I realized I had had enough of dealing with cases and the constant changes at work. Now, the New Orleans office was closing down and moving to Houston.

When it closed permanently, I was the final person working out of the OPR New Orleans office. ICE HQ personnel arrived to collect the furniture, remove the pictures from the wall, and clear out the office I had maintained for over ten years.

Approximately ten months before the closure, ICE HQ determined that the OPR New Orleans office was necessary and that the OPR Houston office would manage OPR operations for the New Orleans area. OPR is the internal affairs division for DHS/ICE employees, and the OPR New Orleans office was a small office covering five states. Due to the proximity of OPR Houston, it was decided to consolidate certain offices in various regions across the country.

I could continue working instead of retiring, with a temporary assignment at the Houston OPR office, where I would conduct investigations. The initial plan was to transfer my position to the ICE HQ office. This would have allowed me to work remotely from my home in Amite and travel to HQ for business as needed. However, my concern was the requirement to perform

HQ functions, which included supervising other OPR offices nationwide. Therefore, I decided to retire.

With the OPR New Orleans office closing, I had to report to Houston before being transferred to HQ, and that's when I said it was time. I always said I would know when the time would come for me to check out. The time came, and I knew it was time to move on.

At that juncture, I realized I had not died yet and wondered if I was prepared for retirement. Just like that, I am considering retirement. Why didn't I attend those retirement seminars or discuss retirement with anyone? What do my retirement figures look like? I sure didn’t know because I never reviewed them.

I had not envisioned reaching this stage, as I had expected to have passed on, with Linda relying on my life insurance.

Here I am, planning to retire, yet I know nothing about what I'm doing. Once it finally sunk in, I had to get to work. Where am I in the retirement stage? Did I do anything to prepare at all? I began researching through the Human Resources department in Dallas, asking them numerous questions. They were extremely helpful in setting me up and showing me what I have available.

The more I investigated retirement, the more I recognized that I was better prepared than I thought. The realization gave me greater confidence about retiring. It turned out that when I was first hired by the government in May 1988, while preparing my employment and retirement documents with Border Patrol, I had already prepared myself for retirement and had the government allocate the maximum amount for both retirement and savings. That was a very astute move on my part, although I wasn't aware of what I was doing then.

I comprehensively understood my retirement situation and submitted my retirement papers to Human Resources in Dallas in September 2022. I advised them that my retirement date was set for December 31st. I cannot explain what it felt like for me that day when I submitted those papers. Part of me felt disappointed because many people in upper management counted on me to get things done, and I thought I was letting them down by retiring. There was also a part of me that felt excited, but one thing was for sure, this feeling I had was so mixed that it was unexplainable.

Moments after submitting the retirement papers, I wanted them back, thinking I had made a mistake. I found myself avoiding my computer so I wouldn't do something foolish and request their return. I did it; it was over, and I was retiring.

I found myself constantly on the move, staying busy, and doing everything possible to avoid thinking about retirement. I wish I had a dollar for every time I said, "What have I done?" But I knew it had to be done; it was time. What kept me in amazement was, "I never saw it coming." Retirement crept up quickly, and I wasn't supposed to retire.

December 30, 2022, was approaching, coming faster than I wanted or realized. With reality sinking in, I began preparing myself. I started closing out my cases, transferring projects to the Houston office, and preparing to return my government vehicle to the OPR office in Houston. I was assigned a new 2022 Jeep Cherokee, a nice vehicle. The vehicle facilitated my travel throughout the five states within my area of responsibility.

Retirement Party in Houston

On December 9, 2022, the Special Agent in Charge (SAC), Jennifer Huerta, Assistant Special Agent in Charge (ASAC) Duane Cottrell, and OPR Resident Agent in Charge (RAC) Jason Dragon hosted a retirement luncheon in Houston.

On December 9, 2022, OPR SAC Huerta, OPR ASAC Cottrell, and OPR RAC Dragon presented me with an appreciation plaque for exceptional and meritorious service as an OPR New Orleans/Houston Senior Special Agent. OPR Special Agents, OPR SAC Central personnel, former colleagues, family, and friends were in attendance. Many stories, laughs, and even a few tears were shared.

SAC Huerta said, "SSA Smith will retire as an SSA assigned to ICE OPR Houston, TX, on December 31, 2022. His efforts and significant contributions have been key to the continued success of OPR Investigations. We thank you, Donnie, for a well-done career and wish you the best in the years ahead. Enjoy retirement!"

Retirement was initially awkward for me, and adjusting to not having a specific schedule or reports to submit took some time. After a few weeks in retirement, it was nice to go where I wanted, when I wanted, and do whatever I wanted. Slowly, I started to get annoyed by anything and everything, and I missed not having somewhere to go, the work responsibilities, and many deadlines to keep. I missed work, and I wanted to go back so badly.

Being around the house was good for a while, but I needed more. I volunteered at the Methodist Church in Amite, performing minor repairs and maintaining the exterior lawn care. I found myself at the church almost every day, for four to five hours, to stay busy doing something. I enjoyed doing all the miscellaneous items around the church, keeping everything up to date, but it wasn't enough. It wasn't enough that responsibilities and demands were being placed on me.

It wasn't long before I began to question why I had retired.

Everything at work was going well for me, and although there were going to be many changes, I could have managed it better than what I was going through right now. Retirement sucks! I missed that interaction with people, sitting for interviews, and solving that criminal puzzle.

Approximately five months into my retirement, I felt I had had enough and wanted to do some work and get paid. This way, I could satisfy my urge to work while bringing home a check, making me feel like I am still contributing to our finances. I have worked my entire life trying to earn and bring home money. Linda and I worked two jobs when we first got married. While I worked for the APD, I also worked at Kent's Welding on Hwy 51 in Fluker, LA., which is located about eight miles North of Amite. I worked for APD at night and Kent's in the mornings.

I worked hard and constantly to make money for us to live on. I worked hard and put in the hours, and I remember thinking how I would keep doing this. But when I saw what Linda was going through, trying to keep our heads above water and pay bills by borrowing from one credit card to pay another, that kept me motivated and inspired me to keep going. I tried hard to ease the burden she was going through, and I know she didn't tell me everything about her bills and money issues because she didn't want to worry me with them. She knew I was trying, and I knew what she was going through.

My retirement was not about the money, and I realized I would have a steady income. I have my retirement, Social Security, Thrift Savings, and Linda's Social Security. Receiving all of this was equivalent to what I earned before I retired. All my investments and thrift savings were gained for me, and we never had to touch any of that money.

In truth, financial necessity was not the primary motivator. I had a steady income from my retirement, Social Security, and Linda's Social Security, which equaled my pre-retirement earnings. All of my investments and thrift savings plan remained untouched. Therefore, seeking employment was more about psychological fulfillment. I believed that achieving this goal would enhance my self-worth.

I realized that I had several opportunities to work. For the government, I was offered a position as an investigator conducting background investigations for new hires and security clearance investigations. I considered the position closely but needed a break from conducting investigations and writing detailed reports. I wanted to do something to stay busy and feel like I was still contributing to my family's well-being.

Harbor Freight

One day, while riding around Amite and thinking about job opportunities, I noticed a Harbor Freight Tools store coming to Amite. I am a huge fan of Harbor Freight and frequently visit the store in Hammond. I drove by the location where the store was coming, and I noticed a website where you could apply for an employment position. I copied down the site and went home to apply for one of the positions. It wasn't 20 minutes after applying that I received a notification to take an online test and answer a few questions.

The next day, Jennifer, the future store manager, called me to ask if I wanted to interview for a position at the Amite store, to which I agreed. (Pictured above is Linda, Me, and Jennifer.)

I had an interview scheduled to meet Jennifer at the Hammond Harbor Freight store. I attended the meeting, which lasted approximately fifteen minutes. Afterward, I was hired upon the completion of my background check. About two weeks after my interview, I started work at Harbor Freight in Amite, three to four days a week for 12 to 20 hours. Working keeps me busy and fulfills my psychological desire to work.

I love working at Harbor Freight because I meet many friendly people, including some old friends I haven't seen in years, and even reconnect with family members I haven't been in touch with in a long time. I work at the checkout frequently and walk around the store to help people in need and assist with replenishing merchandise on the sales floor.

Working in retail taught me a lot, as I had no experience in that field. I also wondered when I was first hired how long it would take for Jennifer to realize my inability to handle retail and fire me. I quickly picked up everything and excelled as a part-time sales associate. I was often commended for my work performance and formed lasting relationships with coworkers.

It is often exceedingly difficult to keep my mouth shut and refrain from reprimanding some of these shoppers. Some people enter the store with an attitude, often over the price of an item or the wait at the checkout. They will express their attitude toward you at the counter when they reach you. But I do my best and haven't knocked anyone out yet!

Jennifer is a remarkable person in her own right. She loves animals and she treats everyone fairly. Jennifer is the type of person the federal government could use more of in management.

Again, retirement crept up on me because, in my mind, it was not supposed to happen. It was also around October 2022 that HQ notified me that I would be reassigned to the DHS/ICE HQ in Washington, DC, effective January 1, 2023. Although I would be assigned to HQ, I could still work from home in Amite. I had no desire to work for HQ again and be a supervisor. I loved being an investigator, and it was time to move on if I couldn't be one.

After writing this and reflecting on everything, I have no regrets about my decision to become a police officer with the Amite Police Department in 1976. Amite PD prepared me for my career because it was there that I realized that this was what I wanted to do.

For pure sanity's sake, I work part-time at Harbor Freight in Amite and do miscellaneous projects around my house, so you can trust me when I say, "I never saw it coming!"

Afterword

I wrote this book to inform my family members and friends about my forty-six-year career in law enforcement. The book explains how I got started in my career, the places where I worked, and a brief description of the positions I held. I also wrote about stories involving my family, who experienced my adventures.

This book is a beginning, and the following books will provide more detailed information about my positions and the types of cases I have investigated.

My next book will be about working for the Amite (APD) and

the Baton Rouge City Police Department (BRPD). It will explain the cases and types of work I performed with both departments in great detail.

The book will be called "I Was A Police Officer," working for the Amite and Baton Rouge Police.

Through "I Was A Police Officer," I will explore the differences between working the streets in a small town and a large city, working undercover as a narcotics agent and a burglary detective. I rode motorcycles for the BRPD and will explain my experiences performing that duty.

I plan to write about my entire career in a series of books, so if you are interested in following my adventures, keep an eye out for "I Was A Police Officer," then the continuing series to follow.

I plan to write about all my law enforcement positions, including working for the U.S. Border Patrol Agent and Special Agent with the federal government.

I hope you enjoyed reading this book, and be on the lookout for those to follow.

Made in the USA
Monee, IL
04 November 2026

67380103R00174